CONTENTS

Lesson 1	Taking measurements	
Lesson 2	Measuring a client	
Lesson 3	Making the pattern The wig	
Lesson 4	Making the pattern The toupee 1, Polythene templat	
Lesson 5	Making the pattern The toupee 2, Paper pattern	
Lesson 6	Making the pattern The semi transformation	
Lesson 7	Making the pattern Knotted hairpieces	
Lesson 8	Making the pattern Facial postiche	32
Lesson 9	Foundational postiche	35
Lesson 10	Knotting	38
Lesson 11	Bracing	47
Lesson 12	Positional springs	51
Lesson 13	Tension elastics	55
Lesson 14	Foundational postiche The wig	58
Lesson 15	Foundational postiche The full transformation	64
Lesson 16	Foundational postiche The semi transformation	70
Lesson 17	Foundational postiche The toupee	73
Lesson 18	Foundational postiche The chignon	77
Lesson 19	Foundational postiche The fringe	81
Lesson 20	Foundational postiche Facial postiche	86
Lesson 21	Partings	89
Lesson 22	Cleaning postiche	92
Lesson 23	The cutting of postiche	95
Lesson 24	Setting and dressing postiche	98
Lesson 25	Attaching postiche securely to the head	103
Lesson 26	Using boardwork for fun	107
Lesson 27	Methods of advertising and techniques of selling	109
Lesson 28	Health and safety	112
Lesson 29	Legal requirements	117
Lesson 30	The history	119

below.

D1347957

1992.

9780951908013.

15.99.

679 AND.

(JA. Publications)

059720

Introduction

Wigmaking step by step, part two, takes the reader through all the different stages of foundational postiche – from pattern making to fitting and styling. Each lesson covers a separate topic. The easy-to-follow text and many, many diagrams ensure a clear understanding of the subject matter. Most lessons are concluded by a revision test.

The author demonstrates the versatility of postiche work by incorporating a section on fun postiche – from eyelashes to furry animals.

Aspects of applicable legislation are included, along with basic health and safety requirements. A short history section concludes the book.

Together with Wigmaking step by step, part one, this book offers a comprehensive knowledge of postiche making.
Together, they contain all relevant information, and more besides, for a qualification in wigmaking.

For all your wigmaking equipment and the latest catalogue please contact:

Banbury Postiche Ltd
Little Bourton House
Southam Road
Banbury
OX16 1SR
www.banburypostiche.co.uk
telephone-01295 757406
fax-01295 757401
sales@banburypostiche.co.uk

A career in wigmaking

When I am asked "What is wigmaking?" I answer that it is not simply making wigs. I prefer to call it, as do many others, boardwork.
No! Not because I find it boring – I find it extremely enjoyable.
I consider the term boardwork more appropriate for two main reasons:

1   The person who carries out this work, works at a bench or board.

2   It is the art of making added hair pieces – anything from a pair of eyelashes to a full wig.
    So what can you do with this knowledge?

Many people think that the work available for a person in this career is limited.
I think you will be very surprised at the number of jobs that are available to the boardworker:

1   Working for a commercial company.
    These companies have specialists in the various stages of the making of postiche. All types of postiche are made.

2   Working at home as an outworker for a commercial company.
    All stages of postiche making are sent to outworkers.

3   Work is available in wig departments of the major theatre companies, in film and television studios. Most types of postiche can be made on site, particularly facial postiche.

4   Smaller theatre companies use outworkers for this work.

5   Salons employ persons to measure and fit the postiche for their clients, also to carry out cleansing and dressing of postiche. A person doing this work is called a posticheur.

6   Department stores have staff to demonstrate and sell postiche.

7 Remedial work in hospitals. Measuring and fitting postiche to persons who, for one reason or another, have suffered hairloss.
Although some of these are not full-time employment, you will see that there is plenty of scope for the trained wigmaker.

Where do you start?

In one of three ways:

1 By training in a wigmaking company.

2 By enrolling at a college which teaches this subject as part of a course.

3 By enrolling with a college that has an open learning facility for wigmaking.

Where would you go from there?

Perhaps to work as a junior wigmaker in one of the companies, then progressing to a senior wigmaker/supervisor.

Use the knowledge during your everyday work as a salon apprentice.

Perhaps as a trainee within a theatrical company.

Eventually you could own or manage a wig boutique or a wigmaking firm.

Lesson One

Taking measurements

Why is it necessary to take measurements when making postiche?

Put down any ideas you may have.

....

....

....

I wonder if you were correct.

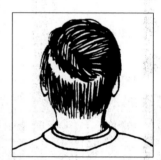

The reasons we measure for postiche are as follows:

1   So that the wigmaker has enough information to make the postiche required.

2   To ensure that the postiche, particularly foundational work, fits perfectly. We've all seen the wig almost falling off a person's head.

3   To ensure that the hair colour used is a perfect match. Nothing looks worse than postiche that doesn't match.

So how many did you correctly forecast?

First of all, I want you to make a record card (sometimes referred to as a wig room order form.

On this record card are noted all the details of the client:

The type and colour of hair
The style required
The measurements of the client
Any abnormalities that may be present, eg bumps or cysts
If possible, a hair sample
If possible, a photograph
The cost quoted
Client's name and reference number
If more than one piece is required
The operator's information, in case further information is needed

Making the record card/wig room order form

Take a piece of card, A4 size (that is, if you do not have access to a pre-prepared card).

Make it out as shown opposite.

You will require four copies of the card.

HANDCRAFTED REAL HAIR WIG/PIECE ORDER

Banbury Postiche

TO AVOID DELAY AND DISAPPOINTMENT PLEASE COMPLETE ALL QUESTIONS
PLEASE ENCLOSE A PICTURE OF STYLE REQUIRED

DELIVERY ADDRESS: If not hospital - state overleaf

ORDERED by (Hospital): .... A/C No.: ....

HOSPITAL A.O.F. attached? YES/NO   DATE: ....

CLIENT Mr./Mrs./Miss./Ms. ....
Address: ....

Age (approx.)	No. of wigs /hairpieces

Postcode: ....   Telephone No.: ....
Repeat Client?   YES/NO ....   Previous Wig No.: ....

Agent: ....   A/C No.: ....
Town: ....   Authorised Domiciliary Visit?   YES/NO ....

FITTING DETAILS - FULL WIGS

1. Circumference   cm/in
2. Forehead to nape   cm/in
3. Ear to ear   cm/in
   over forehead

- HAIRPIECES

1. Indicate position of oilsilk patches/clips
2. Indicate with arrows direction of hair
3. Indicate where hairpiece is worn on head ....
4. Waterproof base   YES/NO

ATTACHMENTS

☐ Enclose a new template/measurements with each order
☐ Enclose a new hair sample with each order

HAIR LENGTH	Front	Top crown	Temples side	Nape	HAIR DENSITY	
	☐	☐	☐	☐	Light	☐
					Medium	☐
FRINGE	Half	Full	Wispy	None	Heavy	☐
	☐	☐	☐	☐		

TYPE OF CURL	Straight	Slight wave	Soft	Medium	Strong
	☐	☐	☐	☐	☐

STYLE DETAILS

Front: ....
Sides: ....
Back: ....

	None	Left	Centre	Right	
Parting	☐	☐	☐	☐	Length .... cm/ins
Crown	☐	☐	☐	☐	How Far Back .... cm/ins From Front
Parting/Crown	Knotted ☐		Drawn Through ☐		

COMMENTS

HEAD OFFICE USE ONLY

PAYMENT

Total payment due ....
Deposit paid .... Date ....
Balance Due ....
Cash ☐   Cheque ☐   Credit Card ☐   Debit Card ☐

BANBURY POSTICHE LIMITED · LITTLE BOURTON HOUSE · SOUTHAM ROAD · BANBURY · OXON · OX16 1SR   TEL: 01295 757400 · FAX: 01295 757401

Patterns are made in different materials. During the next few lessons, you will make patterns in most of the different methods.

Equipment used when measuring, and codes of these items are available at Banbury Postiche Ltd

Eyebrow pencil or waterproof marker	These pens/pencils are used to indicate the outline etc on templates
Polythene sheet	A transparent sheet used for the template base
Paper	The paper must be firm, yet flexible. It is used in the making of patterns.
Transparent adhesive tape	1–2cms wide. Used to strengthen the template and paper patterns.
Scissors (HS1550)	Must be kept sharp and dry.

7

Tape measure (MS2360)	Used for measuring the client's head. Keep the tape wound smoothly.
Tracing paper	Used when making patterns for facial postiche, eg moustache.
Workroom order form	Records the measurements and requirements of the client. It is duplicated and numbered.
Pen/pencil	To record the information.

Revision test

Workroom order forms

1 What is the main reason for a workroom order form?

....

2 List four different items included on it

....

....

....

....

3 Why do we include a hair sample with the workroom order form?

....

....

....

....

4 Why is a photograph helpful to the wigmaker?

....

....

....

....

5 What is meant by abnormalities?

....

....

....

....

6   List three different measurements taken.

....

....

....

....

7   Why is a workroom order form numbered?

....

....

....

....

8   What parting details are listed?

....

....

....

....

9   Why is the salon operator's name and number listed?

....

....

....

....

Lesson Two
Measuring a client

In this lesson, you will learn how to measure your client.
You will require the services of a very good friend.

After reading through the theory section, measure your client and transfer the measurements onto one of your wig room order forms.

The work in this lesson should take between half an hour and three quarters of an hour.

When all the work has been completed, carry out the revision test that follows.

Measuring your client

The approach to the client is most important. Imagine, for a moment, a young person who has been involved in a road accident. He/she has been badly disfigured and has lost most of his/her hair. The result is that the person does not want to go anywhere or do anything – all confidence is lost.

In cases such as these, wigs etc are available on the National Health Scheme. A doctor has to recommend a hairpiece. As you will understand, the way a representative of the wigmaker approaches the client can either make or break the effects that could be gained. Therefore, when measuring a client, a quiet, confident manner is required.

Procedure for measuring a client for a wig

1 Prepare all your equipment as listed in lesson one.

2 Greet your client with the correct approach.

3 Discussion with the client follows.
   Find out the exact requirements of the client
      the style
      the length
      the density and texture (essential if the client has lost all his/her hair)
      whether the hair is to be curly or straight

4 Note all these points on the order form.

5 Fill in the client's name and address.

6 Enter the record number.

7 Prepare your client with a protective gown.

8 Take and record the following measurements:

Circumference (1)
Measure from just above the hairline at centre front (about 1cm in from the hairline).
Proceed around the head, at the same distance in from the hairline and take the measurement when the measure reaches the starting point.

Front hairline (pole) to nape (2)
Measure from centre front to centre back, going over the top of the head.

Ear peak to ear peak, across the front hairline (3)
The ear peak is the point just in front of the ear. Measure from this point to the same point in front of the other ear. Pass the tape along the hairline as you do so.

Ear to ear over the top of the head (4)
Measure from the hairline above the topmost point of the ear, over the top of the head, to the same point above the other ear.

Temple peak to temple peak round the back (5)
Measure from the front hairline at the temple, around the back of the head, to the same point at the opposite temple. It is important that the tape is kept level when measuring around the back.

Temple peak to temple peak across the front of the head (6)
Measure from the front hairline at the temple to the same point at the opposite temple. Pass the tape over the front of the head.

Width of the nape (7)
Lift up the hair. Measure from one side of the nape to the other, using the hairline as starting and finishing points.

Hairline behind the top of the ear to the corner of the nape (8)
Measure from the hairline at the back of the ear, the uppermost point, down to the corner of the nape.

9   Identify any abnormalities that may be present, for example, any bumps or cysts. Likewise, any hollows that may have to be allowed for.

10 If a parting is to be included, identify the position and length required. Note this down on the record card.

11 On the record card, describe the style required.

12 Next, the details of the hair are written on the card. Identify the colour and if possible, attach a hair sample. State the length needed. Give details of the amount of curl (if any) needed.

13 Give the price that you have estimated to the client.

14 State the date quoted for fitting/delivery.

15 Write down if more than one piece is requested.

16 Write your name or reference number.

17 This is then despatched to the wigmaker (in this case you).

Check that your understanding of the position of each measurement is the same as the following diagram.

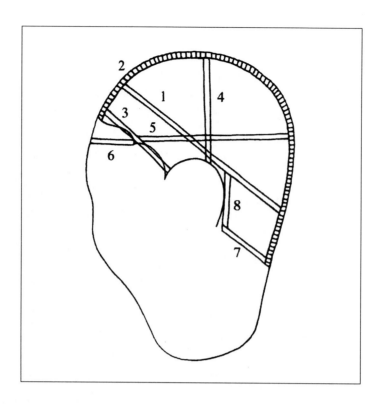

Once you have done so, you should begin again at the start of this lesson, only this time, with your client there for you to measure.

Then answer the revision test.

Revision test

Measuring your client

Without referring to the text or back to your notes, answer the following on a separate sheet:

1   Why is it necessary to have a quiet, confident manner when taking measurements?

2   When the client arrives at a salon, to be measured for a wig, what are the first facts that you must establish?

3   How do you prepare your client?

4   List four measurements that need to be taken.

5   Explain how each of those is taken.

6   On your answer sheet, identify the measurements – numbers 1–8 opposite.

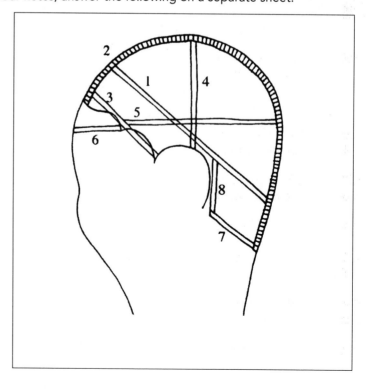

Lesson Three
Making the pattern *the wig*

This lesson takes you through the procedure for making a pattern for a wig.

Equipment used (Items with codes are available at Banbury Postiche Ltd)

Paper, flexible yet firm

Pencil

Ruler

Record card complete with measurements

Adhesive tape

Scissors (HS1550)

This whole lesson, including the revision test, should take about one and a half hours.

Making a pattern for a wig

Follow the step by step instructions. At the end of the lesson you will have produced a sample pattern for your folder.
Have to hand the record card, complete with measurements.
For this stage we need the following measurements:
Circumference
Ear to ear across the front hairline
Nape

Each of these measurements will need dividing into half.
For example, if the circumference is 56cms it will become 28cms.

Method

1   Take a piece of paper which should be firm but flexible. The paper should be the same length as the circumference of your client's head.

2   Fold into half. The fold represents the centre front.

3   Measure in from the centre front, half the circumference. This represents the centre back.

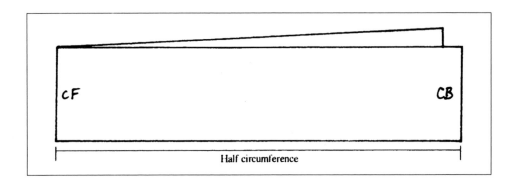

4 Measure in from the centre front, half the ear to ear across the front hair line. This indicates the ear peak.

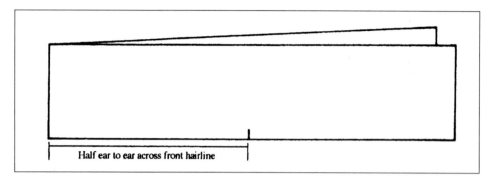

Half ear to ear across front hairline

5 Measure back from this point 5cms.

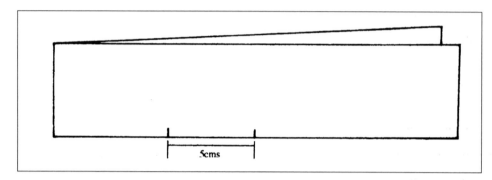

5cms

6 Shape the front hairline.

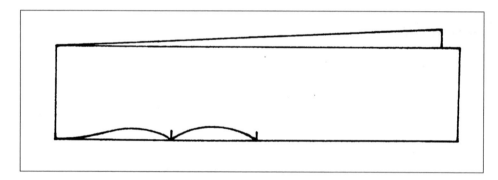

7 Measure in from the centre back half the nape measurement.

8 Measure up at this point 2cms.

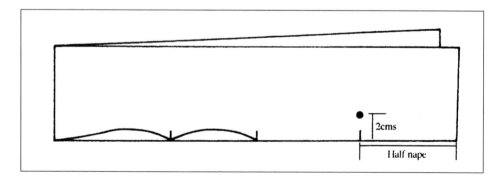

2cms

Half nape

9   Measure up at the ear peak 3cms.

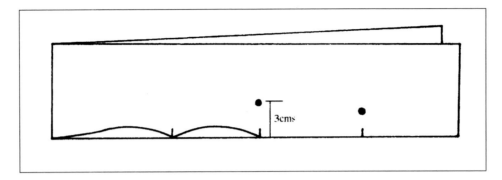

10 Measure up at centre back 3cms.

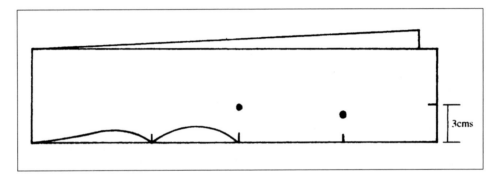

11 Join these together, to shape around the ear and to shape the nape.

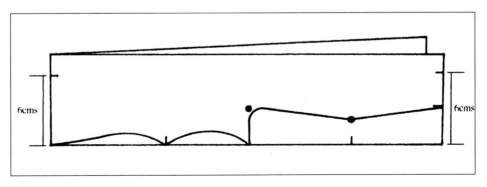

12 Determine the depth of the mount.
This depends on whether or not a parting is to be included.
If there is a parting, then the depth will be the same as the length of the parting plus 2cms.
If there is no parting, the depth is normally 6cms.

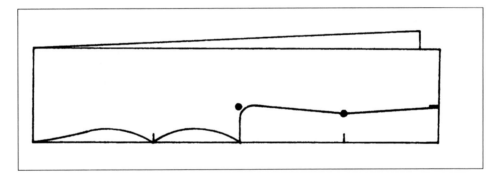

13 Draw in the back line.

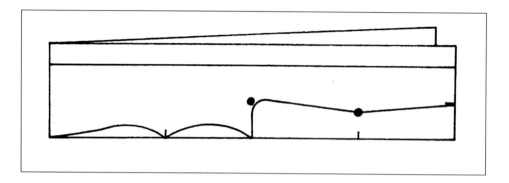

14 Cut out the pattern.

15 Place the pattern onto the client's head to check the fit. Pleat, where necessary. Strengthen the edges with adhesive tape.

16 If the pattern is not to be used immediately, pad it out to retain its shape.

17 You have now made a pattern for a wig.

Revision test

Making the pattern for a wig

Without referring to your notes or to the text, answer the following on a separate sheet.

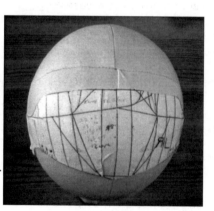

1   List the six pieces of equipment used when making a paper pattern.
2   Why is the record card needed during pattern making?
3   Give three measurements used when making a pattern for a wig.
4   What length should the paper be for the pattern?
5   Draw out the paper after the centre front and centre back have been marked.
6   What measurement is used for the front hairline?
7   Briefly describe how the front hairline is shaped.
8   Briefly describe how the ear peak and the nape are shaped.
9   What determines the depth of the mount?
10 How do we ensure we have the perfect fit?

Lesson Four
Making the pattern *The toupee1 Polythene template*
Lesson four deals with the making of a polythene template for
a toupee.

Equipment used (Items with codes are available at Banbury Postiche Ltd)

Polythene sheet
Waterproof marking pen/eyebrow pencil
Record card
Adhesive tape
Scissors (HS1550)

One hour to one and a quarter hours should be enough to complete this
lesson and the revision test that follows.

Making a polythene template for a toupee

A willing friend is needed for this lesson, or a fellow student.
If you are unable to find a person with hair loss, willing to assist, a block may be used, but the result is
not as satisfactory.

Step by step instructions are given.
If you follow them, you will produce a sample template for your folder and should have no difficulty in
answering the test.

Have to hand a record card.

Method

1   Prepare the equipment listed at the beginning of this lesson.

2   Discuss with the client the exact requirements.

Find out and note onto the record card:

The style
The length
The density
The texture
The degree of curl required, if any

4   Fill the client's name and address onto the record card.

5   Prepare the client with a protective gown.

6   Take the polythene sheet and stretch over the client's head.

NB Avoid the nose and mouth.
Do not let the sheet go too close to the eyes.

7   The corners of the polythene sheet are now twisted firmly.

This makes it mould to the shape of the head.

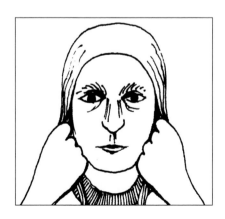

8 Ask the client or an assistant to hold the corners.

9 Place the transparent adhesive tape over the bald area.

The tape should criss cross.

Lay the tape firstly from front to back, then from side to side.

Overlap the bald area by 2cms all around the perimeter.

10 Take the waterproof marker pen or eyebrow pencil and draw in the outline of the bald area.

11 For the front hairline, it is necessary to estimate where the original hairline was. To do this, we look for the one or two hairs that usually continue to grow (they are very fine hairs). If these are not present it is best to consult a photograph.

12 On the template, indicate the following:
Centre front and centre back of the template
Position and length of parting, if required
The direction in which the hair must fall
Position of the adhesive patches

13 Place more adhesive tape over your markings – again in both directions.
This tape makes certain that your markings are retained.

14 Remove the template from the client's head.

15 Wipe the client's head, to remove any perspiration.

16 The template should be reasonably firm.

17 Cut along the outer line. That is, cut off the excess.

18 Re-check the template against the client's head.

19 Pad the template to retain the shape during storage (and in your folder).

20 Check the colour required by the client.
Note this on the record card.
A colour sample is also very useful.

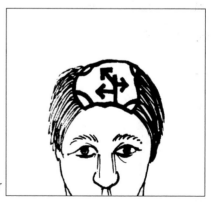

21 Confirm with your client the cost you estimated and the date for delivery. Write down on the record card.

22 State on the record card the number of toupees required by the client.

23 Give the card a reference number.

24 Before despatching to the wigmaker, ensure your name or reference number is written on the card.

Revision test
Making a polythene toupee template

Without referring back to the text or to your notes, answer the following on a separate sheet:

1   List the six kinds of equipment used for making a template of this kind.
2   Give three requirements that must be discussed with the client for the record card.
3   What must you avoid, when placing the polythene sheet on the clients head?
4   What happens when we twist the corners?
5   How is the adhesive tape applied?
6   How much extra should be allowed?
7   What do we use for marking on the template?
8   List four different markings made on the template.
9   How is the front hairline estimated?
10 Why is adhesive tape placed over the markings?
11 When the template is removed from the head, where is it cut?
12 Why is the template placed onto the client's head once more?

Lesson Five
Making the pattern *The toupee 2 Paper pattern*

A step by step guide to making a paper template for a toupee.

Equipment used (Items with codes are available at Banbury Postiche Ltd)

Large sheet of paper
Tape measure (MS2360)
Ruler
Adhesive tape
Pencil
Eyebrow pencil
Scissors (HS1550)

The whole of this section, plus the revision, test should take no longer than one and a quarter hours.

Making a paper template for a toupee
Once more, you will require the services of a willing friend or fellow student.
Follow the step by step instructions to make your sample pattern, then mount into your folder.

Method

Once again, you will require a record card.
List the facts that you will have gained during discussion with your client.

....

....

....

1   Prepare the equipment listed at the beginning of the lesson.

2   Write onto the record card, the facts you found out from
your discussion. (Did you remember all four facts? If not, look back to the previous lesson.)

3   Prepare your client with a protective gown.

4   Using an eyebrow pencil, indicate the front hairline onto the client's scalp.

5   Take a sheet of paper large enough to cover the bald area.

6   Measure from the centre front hairline to the back of the
bald area.

Draw on paper.

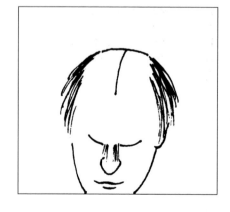

7 Working first on the right of the line, as far as the outer edge of the bald area, measure at 1cm intervals from front to back.

Mark on the paper.

8 Measure at 1cm intervals, working back from the front on the left.

These measurements are from side to side.

Mark on the paper.

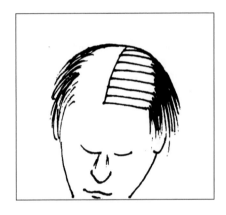

9 By joining up your marks, you are able to draw in the outline shape of the area.

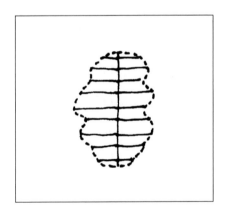

10 Cut along the line you have just drawn.

11 Place the template onto the client's head.
   Mould into shape by pleating the edges where necessary.
   Make any necessary adjustments.

12 Strengthen the edges with adhesive tape.

13 If a parting is to be included, then the position and length are noted on the pattern.

14 Mark the front and back on the pattern.

15 Mark the hair direction.

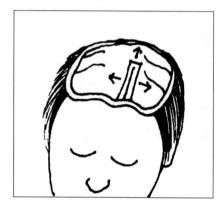

16 Mark the adhesive patches or the position of any clips.

17 Indicate the colour required and/or attach a colour sample on the record card.

18 Indicate, on the record card, the price quoted and the delivery date.

19 Write down the number required by the client.

20 Ensure the client's name, address and reference number are noted.

21 Make sure that the operator's name and/or reference number are on the card before it is despatched to the wigmaker.

Revision test

Making a paper template for a toupee

Without referring back to the text or to your notes, answer the following on a separate sheet.

1 For what reason would you use an eyebrow pencil when making a paper template?
2 Give the three different measurements taken.
3 At what intervals are the measurements taken?
4 Once the measurements have been transferred to the paper, how is the outline formed?
5 What is the procedure for shaping the template?
6 What points are noted on the pattern?
7 Which of the two methods of template making do you prefer? Give your reasons.
8 What is the last item to check before the workroom order form is despatched to the wigmaker?

Lesson Six
Making the pattern *The semi transformation*

The procedure for making a pattern for a semi transformation is explained in this lesson.

Equipment used (Items with codes are available at Banbury Postiche Ltd)
Tape measure (MS2360)
Record card
Paper, firm yet flexible
Pencil
Scissors (HS1550)
Adhesive tape
Ruler

Read through the theory section.
Fill in the gaps as they occur.
Then follow the step by step instructions.
On completion of this lesson, you will have produced a sample for your folder and should be able to answer with ease, the revision test
that follows.

The total time commitment will be about one and a half to two hours.

Making a paper pattern for a semi transformation

What is meant by a semi transformation?

At this point, we need to look back over the work we have done so far.
We have made patterns for a wig and a toupee (two methods).
So let us examine each of those patterns.

The wig
This piece of foundational postiche covers the entire head.
The outer area, from the hairline to about 6cms in, all the way around the head, has a base of a fine net.
The crown area is covered with a much coarser net.
Therefore, the wig is like a cap with hair attached.
The wig has no openings, just a tension elastic to hold it secure.
The wig can be worn to cover total hairloss or just for a change of appearance.

The toupee
This piece of foundational postiche is worn to cover an area of the head which is without hair – usually from the front hairline to the crown (receding hair). The toupee is attached to the head by double-adhesive toupee tape or by toupee adhesive. It is designed to fit an exact area of the head.
In order to understand the semi transformation you will have to consider the full transformation.

A full transformation fits around the outer perimeter of the head.
The pattern used is identical to the pattern for a wig. The main differences are that the full transformation does not have a crown area like a wig and that it does have an opening at the centre back. This is fastened by two hooks and eyes.

So, finally, we come back to the semi transformation.
A semi transformation fits across the front hairline finishing behind the ear on either side.
This piece of foundational postiche has a galloon bind which follows the circumference of the head, fastening at centre back with one hook and eye.

Preparation before making the pattern
1   Prepare all the equipment listed at the beginning of the lesson.

2   Discuss with the client his/her requirements.
    Make note of the style required, the length desired for the finished postiche.
    The texture and density of the hair should be sorted out, as should the curl requirements of the client.
3   Prepare the client with a protective gown.
4   Take the following measurements:

circumference
front hairline (pole) to nape
ear peak to ear peak across the front hairline
ear to ear over the top
temple peak to temple peak round the back
temple peak to temple peak across the front
width of the nape
from the hairline behind the top of the ear to the corner of the nape

See if you can identify each of those measurements on the diagram below, without looking back at your notes.

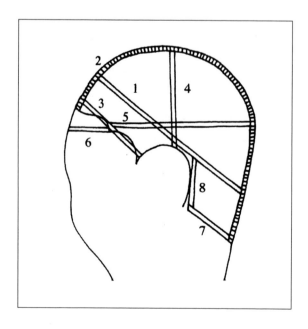

5   If there is any bald area to cover note down the length and depth of the area.

6   If there are any abnormalities present, they must be written down on the

....

....

....

7   If a parting is to be included, the.

....

....

and

....

....

must be noted.

8   A colour sample must be attached or.

....

....

9   Confirm the

....

cost and the

....

Ensure these are written on the client's card.

10 Make sure that the client's

....

and

....

are on the card.

11 Finally, before the workroom order form is sent to the wigmaker, make certain that your

....

and/or

....

is on the card.

Making the pattern

To make the pattern for a semi transformation we need the following measurements:

ear to ear round the front hairline
length of the mount required

Method

1   Take a piece of paper the same length as the mount required.
    This paper should be firm but flexible.

2   Fold into half. The fold represents the centre front.

3   Measure in from the fold (centre front), half the ear to ear round the front measurement.
    Mark with a dot.
    This represents the ear peak.

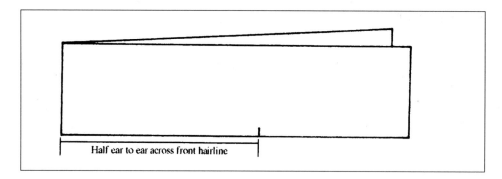

4   Measure in from the fold, half the desired finished length.
    This should be at the opposite end – the open end.

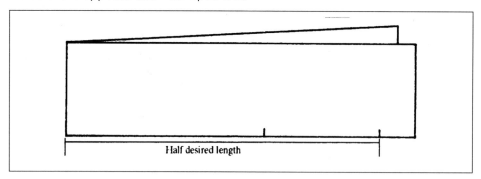

5   Measure back from the ear peak mark, 5cms.
    This point indicates the temple peak.

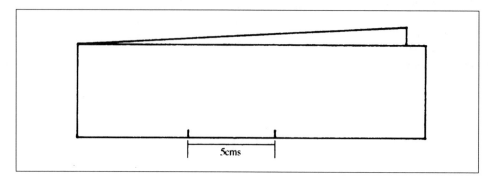

6   Shape the front hairline.

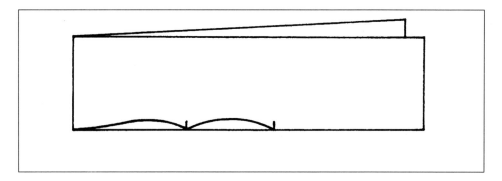

7   Measure up at the ear peak, 3cms.

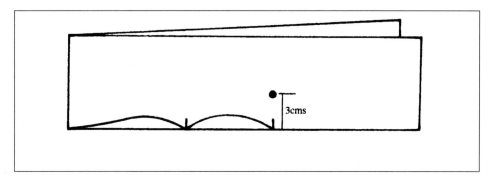

8   Determine the depth of the mount. Consult the record card. Measure
this at both ends of the pattern and join up. NB If a bald area has to be
included, then the shaping will have to coincide with the requirements.

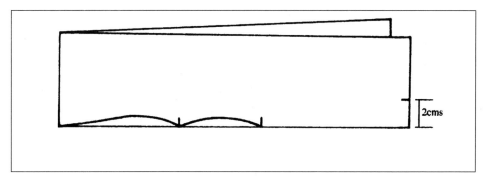

9   Measure up at the open edge, or where your pattern is to finish (if your paper is longer), 2cms.

10 Shape the ear peak and join to the back line.

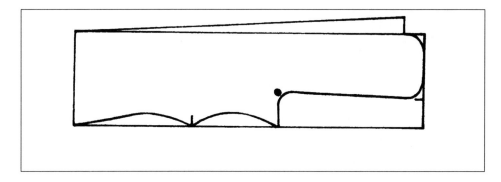

11 Cut out the pattern.

12 Try the pattern on the client's head.
   Mould the pattern to shape, pleating where necessary.

13 Strengthen the edges with adhesive tape.

14 If adhesive patches are needed, they should be marked on the pattern at this stage.

15 Pad the pattern for storage.

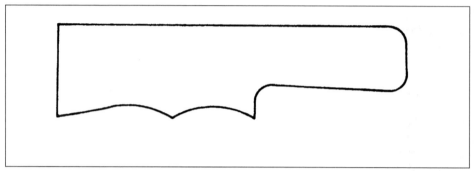

Semi transformation without parting.

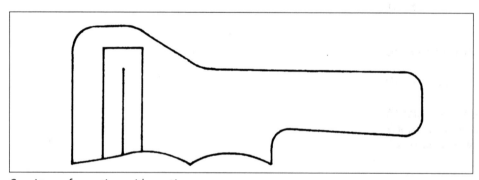

Semi transformation with parting.

Revision test
Making a pattern for a semi transformation

Without referring to your notes or back to the text, supply the information missing from the following statements.

1   A wig fits on the head like a -?-.
2   The crown area of the head is covered with a -?- net, whilst the edge of the wig is made of a -?- net.
3   A toupee is made to fit -?-.
4   The toupee is attached by means of toupee adhesive or -?-.
5   The -?- transformation encircles the head without covering -?-.
6   The -?- transformation fits -?-.
7   When making a pattern for a semi transformation, you need the measurement for the ear to ear around the front and the -?-.
8   The pattern for the -?- transformation is the same as that for a -?-.
9   The fold of the paper for the pattern represents -?-, whilst the open end is the -?-.
10 The front hairline is shaped using the -?- measurement.
11 When the outline has been drawn out the pattern is -?- and -?-.
12 Pleating may be necessary to -?-.
13 The edges are then -?-.

28

Lesson Seven
Making the pattern *Knotted hairpieces*

Chignon (pronounced 'sheen-yon') or similar

Pattern making for smaller pieces of foundational postiche is covered in this lesson.

Equipment used (Items with codes are available at Banbury Postiche Ltd)

Paper
Tape measure (MS2360)
Pencil
Adhesive tape
Workroom order form/record card

After reading through the theory section of lesson seven, make a pattern for a chignon and mount it into your folder.

This lesson and the test that follows should take no more than three quarters of an hour.

Making the pattern for a knotted chignon

What is a chignon?
A chignon is a small piece of postiche.

How is a chignon made?
It can be either woven or knotted.

Where is a chignon worn?
The chignon is normally worn on the crown of the head, but it can be worn in the nape or at any point in between.

Why is a chignon worn?
This type of hairpiece is usually worn to enhance the dressing.

When a client decides that she would like a chignon, she has usually discussed it first with her hairdresser.
Often it is required for some special occasion.
The type of piece needed will depend on the style that is planned.

Method

1   Discuss with the client her requirements.
Establish the length required.
Find out if the hair should be curled or not.
If it is to be curly, then to what degree.
Discuss the colour.

2   Note all these details down onto a record card.

3   During your discussion with the client, find out the intended final dressing.

4   Check the position that the chignon is to be worn.

5   Establish how she wishes to attach it to her head, comb, clip or loops.

6   Protect the client with a protective gown.

7   Measure the area to be covered, both vertically and horizontally.

8   Note down these measurements.

9   Transfer the measurements to a piece of paper and draw in the outline.

If the hairpiece finishes at part of the hairline, then this must be shaped accordingly.

10 Try the pattern in position on the client.

11 Mould into shape, pleating the paper where necessary.

12 If pleats have been necessary, then strengthen the outer edge with adhesive tape.

13 Using a pencil or marker pen, indicate the direction the hair is to fall in the final dressing.

14 Find out the weight that the client would like the final piece to be.
    Write this down on the record card.

This is a very important point.

If a client has extremely fine hair, she will not want a heavy hairpiece.

15 Make sure that the price quoted and the date for delivery is written on the record card.

16 The client's name and address is written onto the card.

17 Give the card a reference number.

18 Write your name and/or reference number on the card.

19 Despatch the workroom order form/record card to the wigmaker.

Study carefully the two different pattern shapes shown here.

Note the instructions that are written on the patterns.

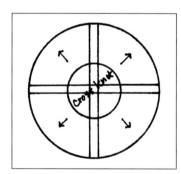 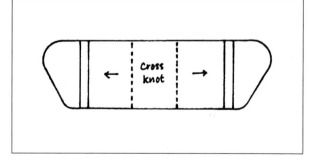

Now you have read the text, see if you can make a pattern for a chignon, to the instructions below, without using your notes.

The final hairpiece will be worn as a cascade of curls flowing down from the crown.

Revision test
Pattern making for a chignon

Without looking at your notes, or back to the text, answer the following on a separate sheet:

1   How is a chignon attached to the head?

2   What type of measurements are used for a chignon pattern?

3   List three points which must be on the workroom order form.

4   Why is the direction of hairfall noted on the pattern?

5   What is a chignon?

6   Where is a chignon worn?

7   Where does the first suggestion to have a chignon come from?

Lesson Eight
Making the pattern *Facial postiche*

The making of facial postiche is the subject of this lesson.

Equipment used (Items with codes are available at Banbury Postiche Ltd)

Workroom order form/record card
Tape measure (MS2360)
Tracing paper
Eyebrow pencil

Read through the notes on pattern making for a beard and a moustache.
Follow the step by step instructions for making the patterns.

This should take no more than thirty minutes.

Finally, in this section, fill in the gaps in the revision passage
that follows.

Making the patterns for facial postiche

When we talk about facial postiche, what do we mean?
Facial postiche are small pieces of added hair worn on the face.
They include items such as sideboards, beards and moustaches.

Who makes this type of postiche?
Postiche of this type is worn mostly for theatrical performances but can be worn for disguise
or to cover disfigurement.
There are firms which specialise in the making of theatrical postiche.

How is facial postiche attached to the skin?
It is normally attached by double-adhesive tape, toupee adhesive or spirit gum.
During this section, it will be necessary to request, once again, the services of a friend.

Pattern making for a beard
Method

1   Prepare the equipment listed at the beginning of the notes.

2   Prepare the client with a protective gown.

3   Using a tape measure, measure

a   from under the bottom lip to the centre of the chin

b   from the centre of the chin to the pivot point of the jaw

c   from the pivot point of the jaw to the top of the ear

d   from the centre of the chin, under the jaw, as far as is required

e   the width at this point.

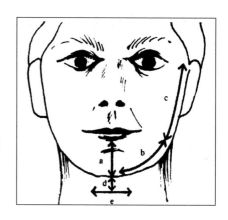

4   Transfer these measurements to a record card.

5   Discuss with the client, the length required for the beard.

6   Establish the texture wanted.

7   Find out whether the client requires it to be curled and if so, to what degree.

8   Note these details onto the record card.

9   Pay special attention to the natural growth line across the cheek and chin areas.

These must again be written onto the record card.

10 Identify the style of beard required.
See opposite for some examples of beard shapes.

11 Indicate and/or attach a colour sample.

12 Write onto the record card, the cost estimated and the delivery date quoted.

13 Make sure that the client's name, address and reference number are on the card.

14 Finally note your name or reference number down onto the workroom order form before it is sent to the wigmaker.

Full beard   Medium full

Anchor   Square cut

Needle   Round/bush

Pattern making for a moustache
Method

1 Prepare the equipment listed at the beginning of this section.

2 Prepare the client with a protective gown.

3 Place a piece of tracing paper over the area where the moustache is to be worn.
Then trace the required shape.

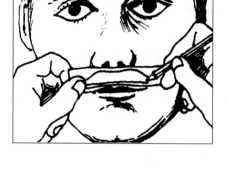

NB It is sometimes helpful to draw the shape onto the skin using an eyebrow pencil, before covering with tracing paper.

4 This then is your pattern for a moustache.

5 Discuss with the client the style of moustache that is required. See overleaf for some moustache shapes.

6 Find out whether it is necessary to have the hair precurled.

7 Establish the texture wanted.

8 Again, the natural growth pattern should be considered carefully.

9 Note all these points on the record card,

10 If possible, attach a colour sample.
If impossible, then state clearly the colour required.

11 Make certain that the record card has the quoted cost.

12 Write the client's name, address and reference number onto the card.

13 Check that your name and/or reference number is on the card.

14 Despatch to the wigmaker.

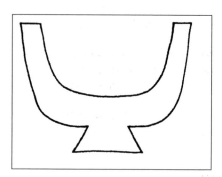

You have now com-pleted the theory of pattern making for beards and moustaches and should also have a beard and moustache pattern for your folder.

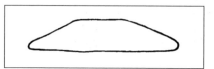

Revision passage on pattern making for facial postiche

Without referring to your notes or to the text, answer the following on a separate sheet.

1 Give two examples of facial postiche.
2 How is facial postiche attached to the skin?
3 In which industry is facial postiche mainly worn?
4 Give three measurements required when making a pattern for a beard.
5 Why must particular note be made of the natural growth pattern?
6 How does drawing the outline on the skin help?
7 What tool is used for this process?
8 Give three details required on the workroom order form.
9 Briefly describe how a moustache pattern is made.

Lesson Nine
Foundational postiche

We have now completed the area of pattern making.
The next step is to learn how to use the measurements that you have taken to make postiche.

Why, you might ask, do we need patterns when we have already made several samples without the need for any pattern?

The answer is that the samples already in your folder are samples of weft made postiche – that is, the hair has been woven onto silks and then sewn into formation. The majority of such pieces are made with no contact with the client. The only details that are required by a wig-maker are the colour, length, texture and degree of curl. Many salons and major stores hold stocks of hairpieces in different colours etc. Weft made postiche can therefore often be purchased 'off the shelf'.

The kind of postiche that requires a pattern is called...

Foundational postiche

Foundational postiche is where a base is made to fit one person exactly.
It is made, therefore, to specific requirements. Once the base or foundation has been made, the hair is then knotted onto it.
Foundational postiche is attached to the head in many ways, depending on the type of foundation and where it is to be worn.
Foundational postiche can be anything from a full wig which completely covers the head, to the smallest moustache. Each has its own method of making.
You will be learning the various methods and the additions that
some of the postiche requires.
You require theoretical knowledge of all the methods.
For your folder you are required to make one of the following:

Semi transformation	Full wig
Toupee	Facial postiche
Chignon or similar	

You will also require samples of the various springs etc.
These will be explained later.
It is an advantage to have a camera to photograph your work at its various stages.

Foundational postiche

The making of foundational postiche has many different stages.
You will find some of the stages very easy and others difficult
to understand.
If you do experience any difficulty in understanding any of the following pages,
do read through them again.
If you are still uncertain, please contact your tutor, as there are many different approaches to the teaching of certain areas.
I hope to have found the most understandable but it is no disgrace to wish to check up with your tutor.

You will need to know the various stages in the making of foundational postiche. These are:

1   The tools and equipment used
2   Preparing the mount
3   The methods of sewing the mount
4   Making and attaching positional springs
5   Making and attaching of tension elastics
6   The use and positioning of adhesive patches
7   Different methods of knotting and their uses

The first area we are going to study is the one which covers the tools and equipment used. I will tell you when each is used and on what type of material. Then you will learn how to use them. Certain items of equip- ment in this section require great care during their use.

Following that, we are going to jump to 7, the different methods of knotting and their uses. You will need samples of each of these knots.
Some can be carried out on your final piece. The others will be mounted separately.

It is preferable to master the art of knotting before you make your final piece. You will then learn how to carry out one of the processes used when making your mount.

The following two sections will cover the making and uses of positional springs and tension elastics.

Finally you will progress through the methods of making different types of postiche.

Tools and equipment used in the making of foundational postiche
(Items with codes are available at Banbury Postiche Ltd)

Wooden block (MS2170)	This is a solid block of wood shaped like a head. Blocks are made in various sizes. It is on this block that the foundational postiche are made.
Adjustable block holder/block cradle (BH1330/MS2250)	This is used to hold the block in position whilst working.
Chin block (MS2190)	This block is shaped like a chin, therefore it is smaller. It is used in the making of facial postiche.
Foundation net (WN2570)	A stiff net which is used for most foundational work.
Caul net/wig net (WN2680)	A much coarser net which is flexible and open spaced (larger holes). This net is used on the crown of a wig only.
Hair lace (WN2575)	A very fine lace net of hair which is used for facial postiche.
Parting silk	Used in the making of drawn through partings
Oiled silk and substitutes (WN2660)	This protects the net from adhesive. It is used on the underside of toupees
Galloon (WG2491-2501)	A plain silk or nylon ribbon which comes in a variety of widths. The galloon is used to outline foundational postiche and for the circumference bind.
Block points (MS2280)	These are similar to headless nails. They are used for attaching the galloon and net to the wooden block.
Hammer (MS2290)	A small hammer used to knock block points into the block.
Pliers (MS2300)	Used for bending and removing block points from the block.
Finger shield (MS2310)	Used when sewing on the wooden block to pick up the point of the needle.

Sewing needles (MS2330)	Used when stitching the galloon and net etc.
Sewing thread/ nylon thread (MS2210)	This must match the net, galloon, hair lace etc.
Tension elastics	Used in the nape of the neck to hold the postiche firmly.
Positional springs (MS2400)	Used to hold the postiche firmly and comfortably against the head.
Adhesive tape (TA1050)	Used to hold the postiche firmly in position on bald areas.
Thimble (MS2320)	Protects the finger during sewing.
Knotting hooks (KH2740)	Available in different sizes. Used to attach the hair to the net. These must be handled with extreme caution. Never leave lying around. Store in a covered container with all the hooks together.
Knotting hook holder/handle (KH2715)	Holds the knotting hook whilst working.
Malleable block (WB1700-1880)	A canvas block which has been stuffed with cork. It is used when underknotting and dressing postiche. Available in different sizes.
Chinagraph pencil	Used to transfer the measurements taken, (for example, beard) onto the chin block.
Transparent	This is used to cover the outline of adhesive tape the pattern on the chin block, thus making certain that the hair lace is not marked.

Store all equipment carefully and in safety.
It is important that the equipment is stored where it will remain dry.

Lesson Ten
Knotting

Contained within this section are the different types of knots. You will learn how to carry out each one and where each is used. The reasons for the different knots are explained.

The following equipment will be required (Items with codes are available at Banbury Postiche Ltd)

Knotting needle (KH2740)   Drawing Mats (DM2880)
Knotting needle holder (KH2715)   Hair (HF3100-3125)
Stiff foundation net (WN2550)   Wooden block (MS2170)
Caul or Foundation net (WN2680)   Block points (MS2280)

Progress through the theory aspect should be reasonably short but you will need to keep going through the notes until you master the art of knotting.

When you have completed a sample of single knotting, a square 3cms double knotting and a sample directional knotting, carried out as a knot-ted parting, complete the revision section that follows.

Knotting

What is meant by the term knotting?

Knotting is the art of fixing hair onto a net foundation.
Knotting gives a more natural result than weaving, particularly when a parting is requested by the client.

How many different types of knots are there?

Single knotting

Double knotting

Point knotting

Under knotting

Cross knotting

Do not let the number of different knots frighten you.

There are two basic knots – the single and the double.
The three other knots are really single knots carried out in different ways.

Points for consideration before starting to knot

Absolute necessities, when knotting, are a chair and a table of the right height. The table must be in a good light, either natural or artificial, as the work is of a very fine nature. It is helpful to rest your work in a work cradle, sometimes called a box. This cradle helps the stability of the wooden block whilst knotting. Make sure that there are no rough edges which will tug at the net and tear it. When working on very fine net, it is advisable to line the cradle with a towel or cloth.

NB The knotting needle is shaped like a fish hook.

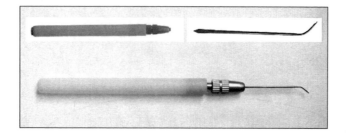

It is therefore extremely important to handle this piece of equipment with care and respect.

Single knotting
This knot is the one used for the majority of postiche.
The only deviations from this knot are when point knotting is required, or when knotting the crown area of a wig where double knotting is carried out.

To carry out your sample, draw a square 3cms onto a piece of paper.
Cut it out a little larger than the square.
Take a piece of stiff foundation net, the same size as the paper you have just cut.
Point these (net on top of the paper) onto a wooden block.

Method

1   Place the hair to be knotted into the drawing brushes, roots protruding.

2   Take a few hairs from the drawing brushes.

3   Turn over about 2.5cms of the hair, root end, to form a loop.

Hold this loop in your finger and thumb.

4   Insert the needle, passing it through one hole, under the bar and out of the next hole.

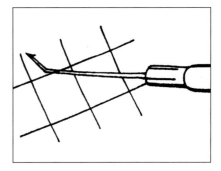

5   Catch hold of 2 or 3 hairs on the hook of the needle.

6   Gently draw these hairs out from the loop of hair about 12mm.

Be careful not to disturb the remainder of the hair in the loop.

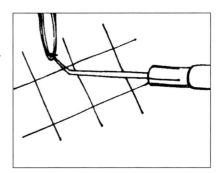

7   Turn the hook downwards and away from you, to prevent the hair from slipping off.

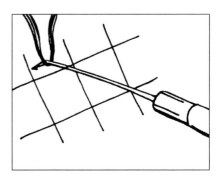

8   Very gently, draw the hook back to its original position.
    Make sure that you have the hair safely caught.
    Do not put any tension on the net.

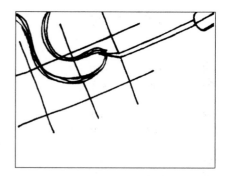

9   Slide the hook forwards a little and twist it about one and a half
    turns. It can then catch some of the hair on the other side of the
    bar, over the top.

    Another method of carrying out this movement is to bring the hair
    around the front and to twist it around the hook. The hook is then
    turned downwards slightly.

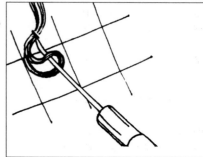

10 Bring the hair that is caught on the hook through the original
    loop of hair.

11 Slide the hair right through the loop and tighten the knot.

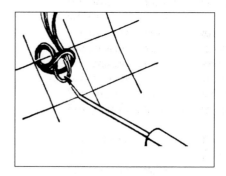

12 The knot is now complete.

Refer to the workroom order form to find out the density of knotting required on the finished postiche.

For your sample, carry out the square 3cms, every other hole, every other row.

When your sample is complete mount it into your folder.

Double knotting
Double knotting is carried out on the crown area of a wig only.

This statement is traditionally true but mention must be made at this point of recent developments in commercial wigmaking.

Wigmaking establishments are now using double knotting for toupee work. Research has shown that the knots are firmer for that type of postiche when blow drying.

The following points of information are relevant to the traditional way of double knotting.

1 The double knot tends to be thicker and therefore not quite as neat as the single knot.

2 The double knot is always carried out on a soft net. This is called caul net or foundation net. Caul net is used on the crown area of the wig only.

3 The knot is much firmer than the single, therefore the double knot is more secure.

4 The double knot is used where security is more important than fineness.

For your sample, you can use the same square 3cms paper that you used for your single knotting.
Cut a piece of caul/foundation net the same size as your paper.
Point onto the wooden block. More block points will be required because of the nature of the net. Do not allow the net to stretch.

Method

This knot begins like the single knot.

1 Place the hair to be knotted into the drawing brushes, roots protruding.

2 Take a few hairs from the drawing brushes.

3 Turn over about 2.5cms of the hair, root end, to form a loop.
Hold this loop in your finger and thumb.

4 Insert the needle, passing it through one hole, under the bar and out of the next hole.

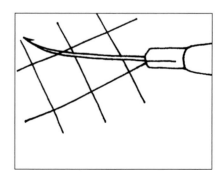

5   Catch hold of 2 or 3 hairs on the hook of the needle.

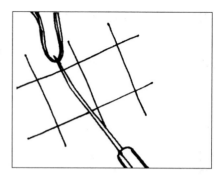

6   Gently draw these hairs out from the loop of hair about 12mm.

Be careful not to disturb the remainder of the hair in the loop.

7   Turn the hook downwards and away from you, to prevent the hair from slipping off.

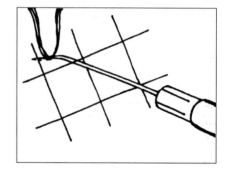

8   Very gently, draw the hook back to its original position.

Make sure that you have the hair safely caught.

Do not put any tension on the net.

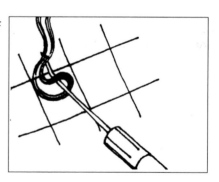

9   Slide the hook forwards a little and twist it about one and a half turns. The hook can then catch some of the hair on the other side of the bar, over the top.

Another method of carrying out this movement is to bring the hair around the front and to twist it around the hook.
The hook is then turned downwards slightly.

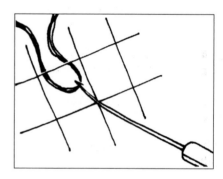

10   Bring the hair that is caught on the hook through the original loop of hair.

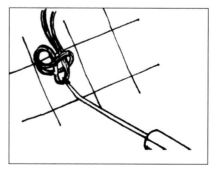

11 Tighten this loop firmly to the net.

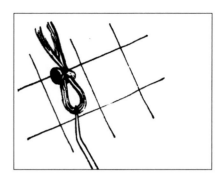

12 Once more, move the hook forward so that it catches hair from the other side of the bar, over the top.

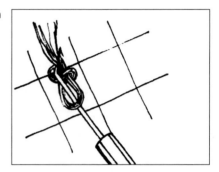

13 Bring the hair through the loop.

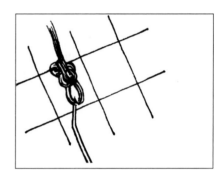

14 Tighten the knot.

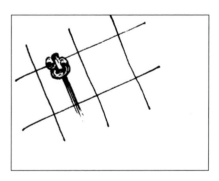

The double knot is now complete.

As you can see, a double knot is really a single knot done twice.
This knot is much harder to carry out because of the softness of the net.
The main points for consideration are:

1 Work in a good light.
2 Make sure that every movement is definite and firm.
3 Tighten each knot as you complete it.
4 Make sure that the loop of hair held between finger and thumb remains firmly held.

The double knot is carried out on every crossover point of the net.

Point knotting

This type of knotting is used when a very short, fine finish is required – for example, if the postiche is to be made short, to sit into the nape of the neck (as in most men's postiche).

Another place where point knotting is used is at the hairline.

The knot is a single knot. The difference is the way the hair is held.

To allow the hair to remain extremely short and fine, the hair to be knotted is placed into the drawing brushes with the points protruding.
The roots are cut off close to the knot, leaving a short, fine finish.

Method

1   Place hair into the drawing mats with the points protruding.

2   Take a few hairs and form a loop, as before.
NB These are the points of the hair.

3   Carry out a single knot as described earlier.

4   Tighten the knot firmly.

5   Cut off the root end of the hair as close as possible to the knot.

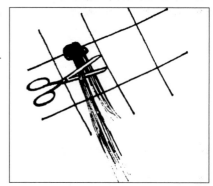

Your sample of point knotting may be carried out on the same piece of net as your single knotting, if there is enough room, other- wise a separate piece of stiff foundation net is required.

A sample about 1cm by 2cms is adequate.

Underknotting

This method of knotting is carried out on the underneath of the mount.
It is used to produce a softer effect around the hairline.
It is also very successful in covering up the edge of the mount.

Method

1   When the main part of the mount, that is the top side of the mount, has been knotted, it is turned inside out and fixed to a malleable block using T pins.

2   After consulting the workroom order form, to establish the way of the natural hair growth, at least two rows of underknotting are carried out.

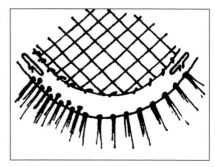

3   Underknotting is done into the galloon which edges the postiche.

4   The knot used is standard single knotting.

5   The hair used is usually quite short and fine.

Cross knotting

This is where the knotting is carried out in opposite directions, to allow a separation to occur, as in a parting. The cross knot ensures that there is no net visible. Cross knotting is also used to give lift to an area of work.
Cross knotting is single knotting carried out either one row in one direction then the next in the opposite direction, or by one knot going in one direction the next in the opposite.

How are we to show cross knotting? In general, the best way is to make a knotted parting. This demonstrates your ability to carry out directional knotting at the same time. Directional knotting is where the hair is knotted so that it falls into a specified growth pattern.

Method
Make a pattern by drawing a rectangle 8cms by 4cms.
Measure down 2cms and draw a line.

Next, make a mark in the centre of the top line and the bottom – that is 2cms in – and draw a line down.
Join the corners with the point
where the lines cross.

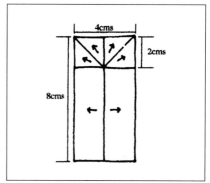

Point the pattern and a piece of stiff foundation net onto the block. Using a contrasting thread, sew, using a running stitch, along the separation lines. Leave the ends loose as the thread is pulled out at the end.

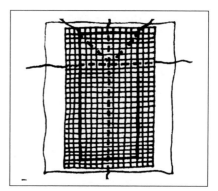

Knotting the parting

Follow the direction indicated by the arrows, when knotting. The hair will then spread out f
rom a parting line.
Knot sections 1 and 2, every other hole, every other line, from the outside, working inwards, until four rows away from the parting line.
The next two rows are knotted every other hole, every line.
The final two rows before the parting line are knotted every hole, every line. The triangular sections are knotted, every hole, in the direction indicated on the diagram.

When this main part of the knotting has been completed, the mount must be cross knotted.

1   Remove the threads.

2   Cross knot the exposed net, one knot in one direction and the next knot in the opposite direction.

Where a parting is required on a finished piece of postiche, the parting is made, then inserted into position.

The parting that has just been explained is called an ordinary knotted parting.

Although it is reasonably successful, net can be seen sometimes.
It is quick to make and therefore, inexpensive.
The appearance is not as natural as the drawn through partings which are explained in a later section.

Revision test

Knotting
On a separate sheet, answer the following questions, without referring back to your notes or to the text.

1   Why does knotting give a more natural finish than weaving?

2   How would you define knotting?

3   What is one of the most important points to be considered before starting to knot?

4   How would you describe the knotting hook?

5   What is meant by a cradle?

6   Name three different types of knots.

7   Which knot is used for the majority of foundational work?

8   What type of knot is most often carried out on stiff foundation net?

9   Fill in the blanks.

A small amount of hair is held in the left hand, after it has been looped at the -?- end.

About -?- cms are turned back.
The hook is inserted under -?-, then a few hairs are -?-.

These are then pulled back -?- the bar.

The hair is once again caught on the hook and -?- through the loop
of hair.

-?- the knot.

10 Define double knotting.

11 On which type of net is double knotting carried out?

12 Give one drawback of this type of net.

13 What is point knotting?

14 Where is point knotting used?

15 What is the main reason for underknotting?

16 Where is it carried out?

17 What is and where would you carry out, cross knotting?

Lesson Eleven
Bracing
This comparatively short section deals with the methods used for holding the mount in position on the block whilst finishing the sewing and during knotting.

Equipment required (Items with codes are available at Banbury Postiche Ltd)
Wooden block (MS2170) with a partially made foundation
Strong, white cotton (MS2210)
Block points (MS2280)
Scissors (HS1550)
Hammer (MS2290)
Thimble (MS2320)
Pliers (MS2300)
Needle (MS2330)

Approximately 30 minutes will be needed to complete the theory section.
This should be followed by a further 10–15 minutes filling in the blanks in the passage that follows.

Bracing
When thinking about the making of foundational postiche, we must consider the way that it is held onto the wooden block during the actual making stage.
The way that this is carried out, is called bracing.

There are three main types of bracing.

Three-point bracing
Running brace
Parting brace

Each one has its own special use.
We shall begin with three point bracing.

Three point bracing

This method of bracing is carried out at the salient points of the head (the representative points on the block, anyway).

If I made the statement, "The salient points are those which are most likely to pull away from the head, when the postiche is being worn," where do you think they could be?

Check your answers.
The salient points are listed at the end of the lesson, on page 84.
These positions are more rounded than the other areas and are therefore more likely to pull away.

If the postiche is not made to the correct shape, then gaps will show.

Method

1   The mount has been made as far as stitching the inner edge of the -?-, which outlines the mount.

2   The net is then turned back to reveal the galloon underneath.

3   A block point is hammered lightly into the wooden block, opposite to each salient point.

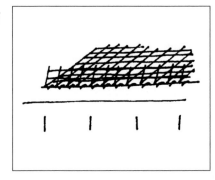

Each is placed about 3cms away from the mount.

4   Take the pliers and turn the end over to form a loop.

5   Thread a needle with strong, white thread.

6   Tie the end of the thread to one of the loops.

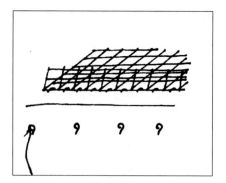

7   Stitch through the galloon, directly opposite the block point.

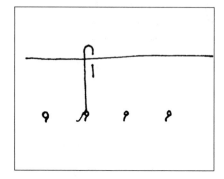

8   Return to the block point and pass the needle through the loop.

9   Next, stitch through the galloon 1cm to the right of the first stitch.

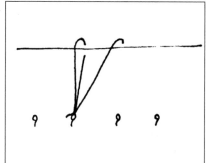

10 Return to pass through the loop.

11 The final stitch is made 1cm to the left of the first stitch.

12 Return to the loop and tie the cotton off, firmly to the loop.

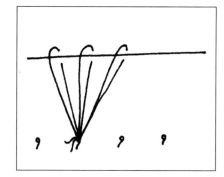

Running brace
Running brace is carried out on the back of full and semi transformations.
It can also be used when making smaller pieces.

Method
After the mount has been prepared, as for points 1 & 2 with three point bracing, hammer a block point every 3cms around the mount, at a point 3cms away from the mount.
The block points are now formed into a loop, using the pliers.

Thread a needle with a length of strong, white thread.
Tie the thread to one of the loops.
Sew through the galloon at a point midway between the two points.
After stitching through the galloon, proceed to the next block point.

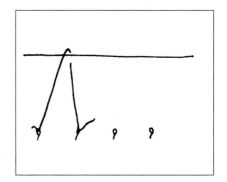

The running brace passes, as its name suggests, from one point to the next, moving round the mount until you come back to your starting point.

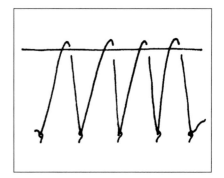

Running three point bracing

What do you think this method could be?

Running three point bracing is a combination of the two methods already discussed. Block points are positioned as for running brace.
The stitching is carried out as for three point bracing.
This is effectively the most secure method of holding the mount.
Were you correct?

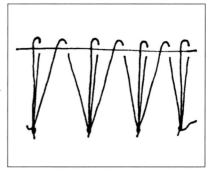

Parting brace

If a mount requires a parting, then this is normally made and inserted after the main knotting has been completed.
When the mount is being made and whilst the initial knotting is being carried out, the parting area needs to be held in shape.
This is done by the parting brace.
The area designated for the parting is held together by a zig-zag or cross stitch.
No block points are required for the parting brace, as the stitching goes from one side to the other.
When the bracing has been completed, the block points that have been holding the work until this point, may all be removed.

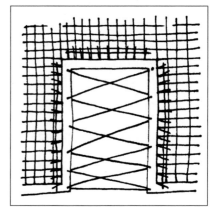

It is a good addition to your folder, to include photographs of the bracing which you will be doing on your final piece. It is not essential, but it adds a nice touch.

Revision passage

Bracing

Without referring back to your notes or to the text, answer the following on a separate sheet.

Bracing is used to hold the mount whilst -?-.

What are the three main types.

Which two of these may be put together?

Together they are called -?-.

The other type of bracing, the -?-, is used at the -?-.

This is required as the partings are made, then -?-.

The small metal pins that are used when bracing are called -?-.

A loop is made by -?-.

The salient points of the head are where the postiche is most likely to -?-.

It is advisable to carry out -?- at these points.

When bracing, a strong -?- is used.

Answers to question on page 78

The salient points of the head are:

The centre front

The nape of the neck

The temple – peak

The ear peak

Either side of the parting

Lesson Twelve

Postional Springs

Postiche must be made to fit.
In the next two sections you will find out the way in which this is done.

Equipment required (Items with codes are available at Banbury Postiche Ltd)

Watch spring or plastic spring (MS2400) Scissors (HS15)
Pliers (MS2300) Needle (MS2330)
File or hard stone Thread to match galloon (MS2210)
Fish skin or polythene Galloon, .25cm, 1cm and tubular (WG2481-2500)
Adhesive tape (TA1050)

The theory section will take approximately 30 minutes.
Follow that by making one positional spring for your folder.
Your other springs will be made along with your final piece.
Lastly answer the revision section that follows.

Positional springs

You might be forgiven for wondering why springs are used.
When most of us think about springs, we visualise a coil of metal which bounces up and down.
Positional springs are not like that. This type of spring is constructed and then moulded to the shape of
the head when it is positioned onto the block. The positional spring retains the shape of the
finished postiche.

Watch spring is the traditional component that is used for making positional springs.
Recently manufacturers have produced a plastic spring which is far superior, as it will not rust.

Historically, whalebone was used in the making of positional springs.
As its name suggests, this type of spring is placed at certain positions.
These positions are called the salient points.

What can you remember about the salient points from the previous lesson?
Write them down on a separate sheet of paper.

Positional springs must be made to an exact fit for the postiche being made.
If they are not of the correct size, they will not be able to do their
job effectively.
The plastic springs are made in different lengths and therefore, do not need to be prepared as watch
spring does. Commercially, this type is more profitable as less time is needed in the preparation.
Positional springs are made after the outer edge of the mount has been stitched with fine blanket
stitches and has been pressed with heated -?-.

Different pieces of postiche require different numbers of springs.

A wig needs nine positional springs.

These are placed as follows:

Centre front	Front to back on the stiff foundation net
Temple peak	A spring is pointed at the relevant and position at the front of the mount. They ear peak are then taken to a point at the back of the stiff foundation net but they must cross on the galloon bind. This is carried out at both sides of the mount.
Nape	A spring is placed at either side of the nape just behind the ear.

Parting	If a parting is included in the mount, then a spring is placed on either side of the area to keep its shape. If there is no parting then these two springs are placed to fan out from the centre front, one on each side.

A full transformation has eleven positional springs placed as for the wig, with the two extra springs positioned one on each side of the centre back opening.

A semi transformation requires seven springs as this piece extends only to just behind the ear. Therefore the nape springs are not needed.

Smaller pieces, for example the chignon, require springs.
The number needed depends on the size of the piece.
Fringes and toupees have springs if there is a parting included.
They are then placed one on either side of the parting.
A circular chignon can have two springs which cross in the centre, whereas a nape chignon would have a spring placed at each side of the nape just behind the ear.

Method

1 Take a piece of watch spring and a pair of pliers.
Measuring against the mount,
in the intended position, cut a piece of watch spring to
the required length.

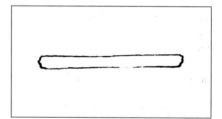

2 Each end of the spring will be rough and will need smoothing and rounding. We achieve this by rubbing on a hard stone or a file. This can take some time so it might be a good idea to have a cup of coffee close to hand, to relieve the monotony.

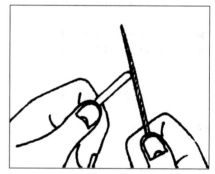

3 To help prevent the spring from wearing through the galloon covering, the ends are now covered with adhesive tape.
The strip of tape should be cut to the same width as the spring and long enough to lie 1cm down each side.

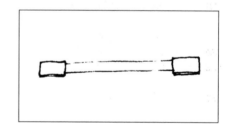

4 Cover the whole spring, next, with a small piece of polythene. (Cling film is an ideal substitute.) An alternative is fish skin. The fish skin is moistened slightly, which makes it supple and sticky so it clings to the spring. Take care to cover the spring once only. If you overlap, it is likely to become bulky. The reason for this operation is to prevent the spring from rusting. When postiche is worn, the wearer may perspire. This moisture could penetrate through to the spring and rusting may occur. This is an essential process when working with white hair as discolouration would happen.

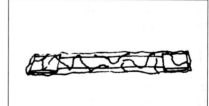

5   The final process is to cover the entire spring once again, this time in galloon.
There are four methods which can be used.

a   Covering a spring with narrow galloon.
b   Covering a spring with wide galloon.
c   Covering a spring using bracing and wide galloon.
d   Covering a spring using tubular galloon.

a   Covering a spring using narrow galloon
A length of .25cm galloon is taken.
The length should be twice the length of the spring plus 1cm.
Fold the galloon over and stitch across the join.
The stitches must be very tiny.
Next sew down either side.

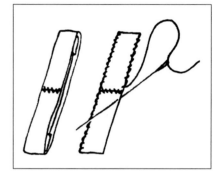

b   Covering a spring with wide galloon
Take a length of 1cm wide galloon the same length as the spring plus 1cm. Fold over .5cm at each end of the galloon and press. Fold the galloon in half along its length and press. Insert the prepared spring.
Sew across the top, down the side and then across the bottom.

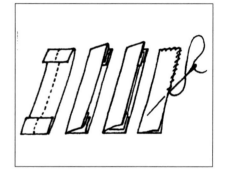

c   Covering a spring using bracing and wide galloon
Again, a piece of 1cm wide galloon is cut the same length as the spring plus 1cm. Using T pins, secure the spring into position in the centre of the galloon, onto a malleable block. Brace the spring to the galloon, using a zig-zag stitch. Fold over the two ends of the galloon. Fold in the two sides.
Sew down the centre and along the top and bottom.

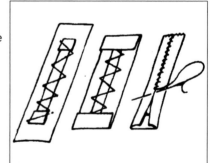

d   Covering a spring using tubular galloon
Take a length of tubular galloon the same length as the spring plus 1cm.
Insert the prepared spring. Turn in the two ends. Sew both ends.

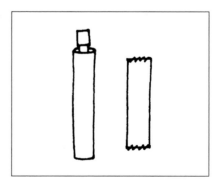

6   The springs are now ready to be sewn onto the mount.
Using one block point at each end of the spring, point the spring in position on the wooden block.

7   Sew the spring to the mount with fine hemming stitches.
Sew all around the spring.

It is the practice of some wigmakers to make the positional springs before starting to make the mount. They then point the springs into position on the wooden block before the galloon bind is pointed into position. The spring will lie next to the scalp.
This means that any perspiration will pass directly to the spring.
Therefore it must be fully covered in polythene or fish skin.

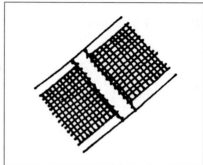

However, there are some very sound reasons for this practice.

1   It is far easier to knot on the net than it is to knot over galloon.
2   Should the positional spring need replacing, then this can be done without disturbing any of the knotting. A much simpler operation and far less time consuming, therefore much cheaper.

Now make one positional spring in one of the first three methods.
Remember to leave one end open for inspection.

N.B. Nowadays however it is common practice to use plastic springs (MS2400) cut to the correct length, as this is easier and eliminates the rust problem.

Revision test

Without referring to your notes or back to the text, answer the following questions on a separate sheet.

1   Why are positional springs used?
2   Which material is traditionally used?
3   What material has been used in history?
4   Where are positional springs placed?
5   Why is it necessary for positional springs to be an exact fit?
6   If the postiche does not have a parting, where are the springs which would normally be at each side?
7   How many springs are needed for a wig?
8   How many springs are needed for a full transformation?
9   Why is there a difference between the answers to numbers 7 & 8?
10 How are the ends of the spring prepared so that they do not wear through the galloon?
11 Why is the whole of the spring covered with polythene?
12 On what colour of hair is this operation essential?
13 Name the four different methods of covering the prepared spring.
14 Describe in detail one of those methods.
15 Explain briefly the two methods of attaching the completed springs to the mount.

Lesson Thirteen
Tension Elastics
This section shows the methods used to make the 'springs' which hold the postiche firmly to the head.

Equipment needed (Items with codes are available at Banbury Postiche Ltd)

Elastic or coiled spring (PC2160)   Thread to match the galloon (MS2210)
Galloon, 5mm or 6mm tubular (WG2501)   Tape measure (MS2360)
Scissors (HS1550)   Malleable block (WB1700-WB1880)
Needle (MS2330)   T pins (HS1460)

The theory section should take twenty to thirty minutes to complete. After you have worked through the theory complete the revision passage that follows.

Finally make a tension elastic and mount it into your folder.

Tension Elastics
Tension elastics are the way that certain pieces of postiche are held to the head.

They are, as their name suggests, elasticated.

The tension elastic is stretched to allow the postiche to be placed onto the head. It then tightens to grip the head holding the postiche firmly against the scalp.

On the introductory page which began this section, I called them 'springs'. This was to make you aware that this item used to be called a 'tension spring'. I make the point so you will know what is being referred to if you research in other publications.

Tension elastics are always placed at the nape.
Tension elastics are sewn either into or onto the galloon bind.

A wig has one tension elastic placed at centre back.
A full transformation has two tension elastics, one either side of the centre back opening.
A semi transformation has two tension elastics, one placed at each end of the galloon bind
at the centre back.
Fringes also have two tension elastics, one placed at either side of the galloon bind at the centre back.

Tension elastics are normally made and then inserted into the wig or full transformation, whereas the other pieces of postiche have mounts made with enough galloon left at centre back to make
the tension elastic.

Method

1   Cut a length of elastic to the required length. This is determined by the postiche being made. An average length is 5cms. At one time coiled wire was used. This had the disadvantage of weakening quite soon. Elastic is far less expensive and more durable.

2   A length of 5mm galloon is cut 1cm longer than twice the length of the stretched elastic. If tubular galloon is to be used, this should be 1cm longer than the stretched elastic.

Covering the tension elastic with 5mm galloon

a   Fold the galloon into half.

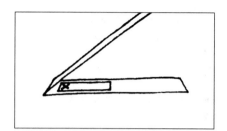

b   Sew the elastic securely slightly in from this fold line on one side.

c   Next, sew the other end of the elastic 5mm in from the end of the galloon on the same side.

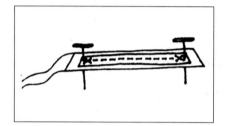

3   Stretch the elastic and stitch at intervals, to even out the tension. It sometimes helps if you pin the stretched elastic to a malleable block.

4   Fold the other half of the galloon over and the two ends in.

5   Finally, sew the sides and end with fine hemming stitches.

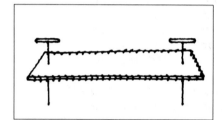

6   Release the tension elastic which will then contract.

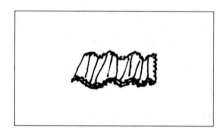

Covering a tension elastic using tubular galloon

a   Slide the elastic down into the tube.

b   Stitch the elastic firmly at one end.

c   Gently draw the galloon along the elastic so that you can stitch the other end of the elastic.

d   Tuck in both ends of the galloon and stitch securely and neatly.

e   Extend the tension elastic, using T pins and a malleable block. Stitch at intervals.

The completed tension elastics
are then sewn into position on
the mount using very fine hemming stitches.

Care must be taken, when sewing the elastic, not to stitch too close
to the edge. Where the sewing is at the very end of the elastic, fraying will occur very quickly.

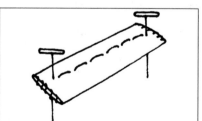

Make a tension elastic after completing the passage that follows.
Mount it into your folder in its contracted position.

Revision test
Tension elastics

Tension elastics are attached at the -?- of pieces of postiche.

They are used to tighten -?-.

A wig has -?- tension elastic, a -?- has two tension elastics.

The tension elastics are placed in the -?- on a semi transformation or fringe.

Tension elastics can be covered using -?- or -?- galloon.

It is necessary to stitch at intervals to -?-.

The galloon is cut -?-.

An average length for a tension elastic is -?-.

The spring should be -?-.

If care is not taken when sewing the elastic -?-.

For this reason we -?-.

How did you get on?

Check your answers against the notes.

I hope you did well.

Lesson Fourteen
Foundational Postiche *The wig*

In this section, I will explain the making of the largest piece of postiche – the wig.

Equipment used when measuring, and codes of these items which are available at Banbury Postiche Ltd

Tools and equipment required (Items with codes are available at Banbury Postiche Ltd)

Completed workroom order form	Thimble (MS2320)
Ready made pattern or pattern	Scissors (HS1550)
making equipment	Nine positional springs (lesson twelve)
Wooden block (MS2170)	Galloon, 12mm,5mm,6mm (WG2491-2501)

Equipment required for making a tension elastic (lesson thirteen)

Caul/Foundation net (WN2680)	Stiff foundation net (WN2550)
Hammer (MS2290)	Pressing irons
Pliers (MS2300)	Hair of the required colour (HF3100-3125)
Block points (MS2280)	Knotting needle and holder (KH2740-KH2715)
Thread to match the hair colour (MS2210)	Drawing Matts (DM2880)
Strong white thread (MS2210)	Malleable block (WB1700-WB1880)
Needle (MS2330)	T pins(HS1460)
Finger shield (MS2310)	Tape measure (MS2360)

It will take you about one and a half to two hours to complete this theory
section. Following, is a revision test for which you should allow yourself thirty minutes.

The making of a full wig is quite a lengthy process to a student.

The Wig

Do you own a wig?

If you do, does it fit perfectly?

Have you ever worn a wig?

Most people have come across wigs at some point in their lives.
It may be that they have been involved in some theatrical production that has made it necessary for them to wear a wig.
The disadvantage with this introduction to postiche is that it rarely fits well.
The wearer then feels uncomfortable.
From then on, the person always assumes that all postiche is uncomfortable.
This is pity, because a properly made wig fits snugly to the head.

When you reach the section on the history of postiche, you will learn how the wearing of postiche has changed over the years.

What is a wig?
A wig is a piece of postiche which covers the whole head.
A cap of net covered with hair.

How do we make certain that the wig is comfortable?
Wigs are made to the client's own measurements.
This means that, as each wig is made to order, the measurements must be exact.
How many reasons can you think of for wearing a wig?
How many could you think of?

Check them against my list below.

Reasons for wearing a wig

1   For a complete change of appearance
2   For fun
3   In television or theatrical productions
4   For fancy dress parties
5   After an accident
6   Where the hair has dropped out following medical treatment
7   If a person suffers from severe alopecia
8   For disguise

Did you think of any more or any different reasons?

Numbers 5 to 7 require understanding and tact, as the client may still be suffering from some illness or from shock.

Because the wig will cover any existing hair, it can be made in any colour. It does not have to match the client's own hair colour unless he/she wants it to.
Let me now take you through the procedure for making a wig.
Reference will be made to work already covered in part one and part two of this book. If your memory fails you, then return to the area mentioned and carry out the revision section. You will be amazed at the amount you really know, but if you are still unsure then read through the whole section again before returning to this work.

Making a wig

1   Prepare all the equipment.

2   Read through the workroom order form.
    Check that you have the right hair colour. If you do not then you will have to mix the hair (lesson four, Wigmaking step by step, part 1).

3   If you have a prepared pattern, then ensure that the measurements match those on the workroom order form. If not, then prepare a pattern (lesson three).

4   Take a wooden block, 2cms larger than the circumference of the head. This extra is taken up by the tension elastics. The crown of the block may need shaping if the client has an unusually shaped crown, eg cysts.

5   Point the pattern into position on the block.

a   Place a block point on the front and back of the pattern at CF.

b   Using the tape measure, measure from CF to CB. Refer to workroom order form.

c   Point the two ends of the pattern in this position.

d   Again, using the temple peak to temple peak across the forehead measurements on the workroom order form, check that the pattern is in the correct position.
    Point at temple peaks.

6   Take a length of 5mm or 12mm galloon and point it around the circumference of the head. Use as few block points as possible.

7   Next, using 5mm or 12mm galloon, outline the outer and inner edge of the pattern. Follow the shape of the pattern but do not fold the galloon. Use as few block points as you can.

8   Where these lengths of galloon join at CB sew neatly, using very fine stitches.

9   A rectangular piece of stiff foundation net is taken. The size corresponds to the required wig. Find the middle of the net and point at CF (front and back and on the galloon bind).

NB It is important to remove the points from underneath, before placing a point through both the net and galloon.

10 Work from the CF round to the CB, removing the points from underneath and then replacing through the net and galloon. This is why we use as few block points as possible. The net may need pleating or moulding to the shape of the block.

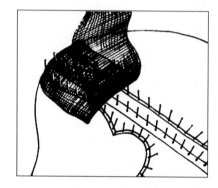

11 The net is sewn together, where it joins at the CB.

12 Both sides of the galloon bind are now sewn to the net. The hem-ming stitches should be very tiny.

It is important to remember that it is the underneath stitching that will be visible when the wig is finished.

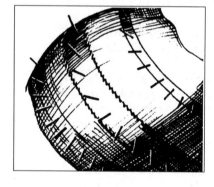

13 Next, the inner edge of the galloon which is outlining the pattern is sewn in the same way.

14 Once this has been completed the front edge is braced. It is usual to use a running three point brace (lesson eleven). The points from this edge of galloon can now be removed.

15 The excess net is now trimmed off. That is, any net which pro-trudes more than three holes be-yond the galloon.

16 Fold under the net, placing the raw edge between the galloon and the upper net, along the front (hairline) edge.

17 Sew this edge using very fine blanket stitching.

18 The front edge of the mount is now complete, so we can turn our attention to the inner edge.
Carefully lift the foundation net up and back.

19 Take a piece of caul/foundation net and place it over the crown area.

20 This piece of net is slid gently between the galloon and the stiff foundation net.

21 Backstitch the caul net to the galloon.

22 If there is any excess caul net, then it must be trimmed off at this point.

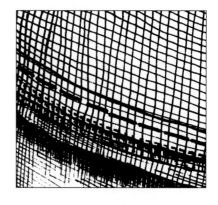

23 The stiff foundation net is then folded under, as you did at the front edge and then sewn to the galloon, stitching through all three layers.
Remove the block points that had held the net in position.

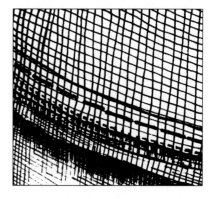

24 Heat up the pressing irons and press the stitching.

You have now reached the stage where the positional springs are made and inserted.
Can you remember how to make them?

How many are required?

Where are they placed?

Were you able to answer the questions? If so, then very good.
If you could not remember all the answers, then re-read through that section (lesson twelve) before carrying on.

The mount is now ready for knotting.
Which methods of knotting do you think will be required?

I wonder if you realised that single, double, directional and underknotting are used.

You did? Great!

General rules for knotting a wig

If there is a parting included, then the hair is knotted to fall away from the parting.

Where no parting is included, the hair is knotted to fall away from the centre front. The block of net 3cms either side of the centre front is cross knotted to avoid splitting.

Start at the base of the intended style and knot up to the top of the style.

This means that the hair which has been knotted will always be below and therefore out of the way during knotting.

Knotting should be as fine as possible.

Knotting procedure

1   Refer to the workroom order form to check the style required for the finished wig.
    This will tell you the direction the hair has to fall. It will also tell you how much hair is required – the density of the wig.

2   The stiff foundation net is then knotted in the direction of the intended style. Single knotting is used.

3   After all the single knotting has been completed, the caul/wig net is knotted using double knotting.
    Again, refer to your workroom order form to find out the direction and the density of hair required.

4   If the mount requires a drawn through parting (explained in a subsequent section), this is made and inserted at this point.

5   The bracing cotton is now cut and the mount removed from the wooden block.

6   Turn the mount inside out and pin, using T pins onto a malleable block.

7   Remove the block points, used for your bracing cotton, from your wooden block and store the block away safely.

8   Return to your mount which is now inside out on the malleable block and carry out at least 2 rows of underknotting into the extreme edge of the galloon.

9   Your mount has now been knotted.

Take a length of galloon and some elastic and prepare a tension elastic.
This was explained in lesson thirteen.

Can you remember the purpose of the tension elastic?

Briefly describe the making of a tension elastic.

....

....

....

....

The tension elastic is sewn onto the galloon bind at the centre back.

The final stage is to prepare the mount for wearing. Turn it the correct way and repin, using T pins, in position on the malleable block. Check once again with your workroom order form for the style requirements.
Cut and style the wig as requested.

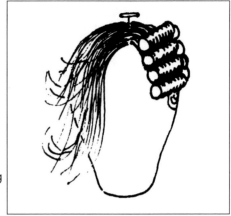

This final stage may be carried out by the posticheur. He/she has access to the client and it may be preferred to cut and dress the wig whilst it is on the client. Cutting and dressing a wig on the client has beneficial points as well as undesirable points.

Points 'for'
Shaping is easier when carried out on the client.
The fit can be checked before styling is done.
Where a wig is required to be short and shaped into the nape, the flow of the hair is easier to assess.

Points 'against'
If the client is embarrassed at having to wear a wig, then to place a shapeless wig onto the client is not very tactful. This type of client is given much more confidence if the effect is instant. If the client agrees, but seems a little unsure, then carry out the shaping and styling without a mirror.

You now have your completed wig.

Without referring to your notes or to the text, answer the following questions on a separate sheet.

1   Give the definition of a wig.

2   What types of nets are used in the making of a wig?

3   Where does the galloon bind sit?

4   What sizes of galloons are used and where are they placed?

5   How many positional springs are needed?

6   Where are they placed?

7   What types of stitchings are used?

8   What different knots are used and where?

9   What size of block is used?

10 Briefly describe how is the wig knotted?

11 Where do you find the information about the required style?

12 How many tension elastics are used on a wig?

13 How many rows of underknotting are used and what is their purpose?

14 Name the two ways of styling the wig.
    Give one point to explain each way.

Lesson Fifteen
Foundational Postiche *The full transformation*

This section explains the making of another piece of foundational postiche.

Tools and equipment required (Items with codes are available at Banbury Postiche Ltd)

Completed workroom order form
Ready made pattern or pattern
equipment
Wooden block (MS2170)
Galloon, 12mm,5mm,6mm (WG2491-2501)
Stiff foundation net (WN2550)
Caul/foundation net (WN2680)
Hammer (MS2290)
Pliers (MS2300)
Block points (MS2280)
Thread to match the hair colour (MS2210)
Strong white thread (MS2210)
Needle (MS2330)
Finger shield (MS2310)

Thimble (MS2320)
Scissors (HS1550)
Eleven positional springs (lesson twelve)

Equipment required for making a tension elastic
(lesson thirteen)

Pressing irons
Hair of the required colour (HF3100-3125)
Knotting needle and holder (KH2740-KH2715)
Drawing Matts (DM2880)
Malleable block (WB1700-WB1880)
T pins (HS1460)
Tape measure (MS2360)

After completing the theory section spend about thirty minutes on the revision exercise that follows.

The full transformation
This piece of postiche fits around the hairline.
It encircles the head as a wig does, but it has no crown area.
This allows the client's own hair to be dressed in with the added postiche.

When would a full transformation be worn?

A client with a receding hairline and who wishes to wear long hair.

If a client has had an accident and the treatment necessary has caused hair loss at the frontal area.

Perhaps a client would like a style where the hair is taken from the hairline to the crown and
then fastened into a chignon effect.
Her hair could possibly be a short bob length, ie all one length, finishing just below the nape.
The only hair that is long enough, is the hair growing on the crown and between the temple peaks
across the front hairline.
The side hair and the nape hair are far too short.
To fit a full transformation overcomes this problem.

To change the colour of the hair at the front non-permanently.

To give more length to the nape hair.

There are two main differences between a wig and a full transformation.
One has been mentioned earlier in this section.
Can you remember it without looking back?
What was it?

A wig covers the whole head, similar to a cap. There is no opening.
The full transformation goes around the hairline and it has an opening at the centre back.
The full transformation fastens at the centre back with two hooks and eyes.

Oh, yes! The difference mentioned earlier.
Did you remember that the crown is open?
This means that no caul/foundation net is used.

You did? Good!

The pattern for a full transformation is the same as the one for a full wig.

Method

1   Prepare all the equipment.

2   Read through the workroom order form.
    Check that you have the right hair colour. If you do not, then you will have to mix the hair.
    (Lesson four in part one.)

3   If you have a prepared pattern, check that the measurements match those on the
    workroom order form.
    If not, then prepare a pattern.

4   Take a wooden block, 2cms larger than the circumference of the head.
    This extra is taken up by the -?-.

5   Point the pattern into position on the block.

a   Place a block point at the front and back of the pattern
    at CF.

b   Using the tape measure, measure from CF to CB. Refer to
    workroom order form.

c   Point the two ends of the pattern at this position –
    the nape.

d   Next, using the temple peak to temple peak across the fore
    head measurements from the workroom order form, check
    that the pattern is correctly positioned.
    Point at temple peaks.

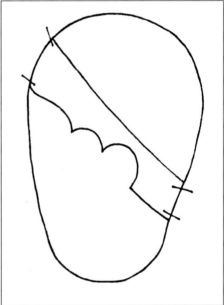

6   Take a length of 5mm or .75cm galloon and point it around
    the circumference of the head. This is the galloon bind. It
    gives firmness to the shape. Use as few block points
    as possible.

7   Next, using 12mm or 5mm galloon, outline the edge of
    the pattern.
    Begin at the centre back.

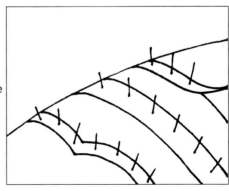

Proceed along the front edge of the pattern, up one side of
the centre back, along the back edge of the pattern and up the
other side of the centre back to meet with the
starting point. Use as few block points as you can.

8 Where this galloon meets at CB, sew neatly, using very fine stitches.
Also, sew the galloon bind to the outer edging galloon where it meets at each side of the centre back opening.

9 A rectangular piece of stiff foundation net is taken.
The size should be just enough to cover the pattern with a small overhang. Find the middle of the net and point at CF (front and back and on the galloon bind).

NB It is important to remove the points from underneath, before placing a point through both the net and galloon.

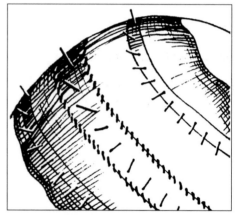

10 Work from the CF round to the CB, removing the points from underneath and then replacing through the net and galloon. This is why we use as few block points as possible. The net may need -?- or -?- to the shape of the block.

11 Both sides of the galloon bind are now sewn to the net. The hemming stitches should be very tiny.

It is important to remember that it is the underneath stitching that will be visible.

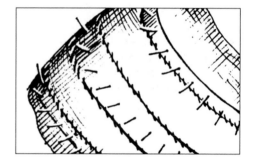

12 Next, the inner edge of the galloon which outlines the pattern is sewn.

All around the inner edge is sewn.

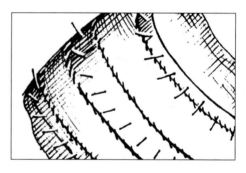

13 Once this has been completed, the mount is braced.

It is usual to use a running three point brace (lesson eleven).

The points holding the mount can now be removed.

14 Trim off any net which protrudes more than three holes beyond the galloon.

15 Fold the net under, placing the raw edge between the galloon and the upper net.

16 Sew around the mount's outer edge, using very fine blanket stitching.

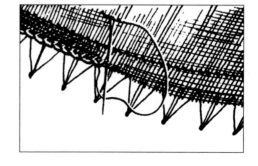

17 Next, we take eleven positional springs.
    If they are not already made, then they must be made and
    stitched onto the mount (lesson twelve).

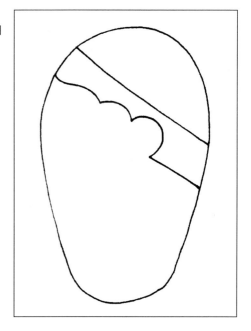

As you, I hope, have realised, this is another difference
between a wig and a full transformation.
The wig has nine positional springs, whereas a full
transformation has eleven. The two extra are placed
one either side of the centre back opening.

Can you remember where the positional springs
are placed on a wig?
Try to fill in the gaps opposite.

Positional springs are placed in the following positions on a
full transformation:

One is placed at the centre -?-.

One is placed on each side of the parting. If there is
no parting included, these are placed to fan out from -?-.

Two more are positioned to cross on the -?-.

They start at -?- and -?- and finish at the back of the mount.

This is carried out on both sides of the mount.

One is placed at each side of the -?- as close to the back of the ear section as possible.

Finally, a positional spring is placed at each side of the opening at -?-.

Eleven springs in all.
Now check your answer with the diagram opposite.
Press all the stitching with heated pressing irons.
The mount is now ready for knotting.
Which methods of knotting are you going to use?

There are three methods.
Yes, I know. By now, you know them off by heart –
single, underknotting and cross knotting.

The general rules for knotting a full transformation
are similar to those for the wig.
Always refer to the workroom order form for the
direction required for hairfall.
Check the colour requested before knotting is begun.
Keep knots fine.
Knot the extreme edge first.
If the mount requires a parting, establish from the workroom order form
whether this is to be made and inserted or whether it is to be knotted in with the main work.
If drawn through, it is best to make this first.

Knotting procedure for a full transformation

1   Refer to the workroom order form to check direction the hair is intended to fall for the finished postiche. It will also tell you the amount of hair required.

2   The mount is then knotted in the direction stated. Single knotting is used.

3   Begin by knotting the extreme edge of the transformation. These knots must be very fine and as close as possible to each other. It is often beneficial to under draw these knots. This means to insert the knotting needle from under the galloon passing up into net.
    The knot then encompasses the outer edge.

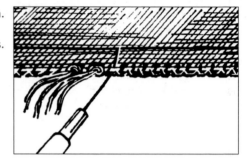

4   Starting at the nape, the base of the style, knot in fine single knotting.

5   Remember that, as you proceed up the sides, you should knot the hair to fall away from the centre front or the parting, if one is included.

6   If no parting, cross knot the centre 6cms at the centre front.

7   Where there is a drawn through parting, it is inserted at this point.

8   The bracing cotton is now cut and the mount removed from the wooden block.

9   Turn the mount inside out and pin, using T pins, onto a malleable block.

7   Remove the block points, used for your bracing cotton, from your wooden block and store the block away safely.

8   Return to your mount which is now inside out on the malleable block and carry out at least 2 rows of underknotting into the extreme edge of the galloon, along the hairline edge.

9   Your mount has now been knotted.

10 Remove from the malleable block and turn the correct way.

Two more items are required before the full transformation is completed.

1   Two tension elastics need to be made and sewn, one either side of the centre back opening, along the galloon bind.

2   Two sets of hooks and eyes are sewn at the centre back opening. These must be positioned so that the hook points away from the scalp.

The mount can now be styled, as directed on the workroom order form.

Revision test
The full transformation

Without referring back to your notes or to the text, answer the following on a separate sheet.

1   Give the number of positional springs needed for a wig and a full transformation.

2   What are the two main differences between a wig and a full transformation?

3   Which type of net is used for a full transformation?

4   What is the name given to the galloon that follows the circumference?

5   How many tension elastics are required for a full transformation?

6   Where are they placed?

7   How is a full transformation fixed to the head?

8   Give two reasons for the wearing of a full transformation.

9   Briefly explain the general guidelines to knotting a full transformation. This lesson explains how a semi transformation foundation is made.

Lesson Sixteen
Foundational Postiche *The semi transformation*

Tools and equipment required (Items with codes are available at Banbury Postiche Ltd)

Record card complete with measurements
Pattern made for semi transformation or pattern equipment
Wooden block (MS2170)
Galloon, 12mm,5mm,6mm (WG2491-2501)
Stiff foundation net (WN2550)
Hammer (MS2290)
Pliers (MS2300)
Block points (MS2280)
Cotton match the hair colour(MS2210)
Strong white thread (MS2210)
Needle (MS2330)
Finger shield (MS2310)
White Cotton (MS2210)

Thimble (MS2320)
Scissors (HS1550)
Positional springs,explained in (lesson twelve)

Tension elastics, explained in (lesson thirteen)
Pressing irons
Hair of the required colour (HF3100-3125)
Knotting needle and holder (KH2740-KH2715)

Malleable block (WB1700-WB1880)
T pins (HS1460)
Tape measure (MS2360)

The theory section of this lesson should take about one hour to work through. On completion of the theory, work through the questions that follow. They should take about 20 minutes. If this is a sample you have decided to make, it will take several weeks to complete.

The semi transformation

What is a semi transformation?
A semi transformation is a piece of foundational postiche which fits around the front hairline. It is dressed in with the client's own hair.

How far back does the mount extend?
It is normally about 6cms in depth, unless a parting is to be included.

How wide is the finished postiche?
The mount is made to fit from just behind one ear across the front hairline to just behind the other ear.

How is it fastened to the head?
The semi transformation fastens at centre back with one hook and eye.
This is fixed to the ends of the galloon bind which encircles the circumference of the head.

Does it fit firmly to the head?
Yes.

The semi transformation has two tension elastics, one at each end of the galloon bind.

How does the postiche keep its shape?
Positional springs, 7 in total, are made and placed at the salient points of the head. These are used to hold the postiche close to the head at the points where it is likely to pull away.

When would a client require a semi transformation?
There are many reasons a semi transformation would be worn.

The main reasons are:
A receding hairline
After an accident

The choice of colour is of the utmost importance as it has to blend in with the wearer's own hair colour. All cotton, nets etc must blend in with the client's hair colour.

Method

1 Take the workroom order form and make a pattern for a semi transformation.

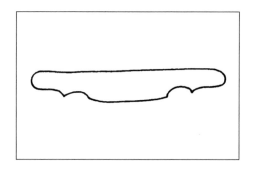

2 Ensure that all the measure-ments from the pattern correspond with the workroom order.

3 Take a wooden block 2cms larger than the circumference of the client's head. This allows for the tension elastics to take up the tension.

4 Point the pattern onto the wooden block. Use the measurements circumference, forehead to nape, ear to ear over crown and temple peak to temple peak across the forehead to ensure it is in the right place. Use as few block points as possible.

5 Make the galloon bind. Point galloon, 5-12mm wide, around the circumference of the head. Allow an extra l0cms on each end at the meeting point so that the tension elastics can be made.

6 Next point 12mm or 5mm galloon around the edge of the pattern. All block points should point outwards.

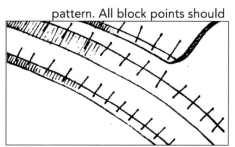

7 Sew the joins, using very fine run & fell stitching.

8 Take a piece of stiff foundation net and point over the galloon. NB It is important to remove the block points from underneath as you progress.

9 The net will require moulding or pleating, to gain the correct shape.

10 First, sew both sides of the galloon bind. This should be in very fine hemming stitches.
It is often helpful to use a thimble and a finger shield.

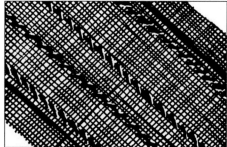

11 Next, sew the inner edge of the outlining gallon with fine hemming stitches.

12 The mount is now braced. This is covered in lesson eleven. Block points are placed, first opposite the salient points, then at frequent intervals in between.
After the points have been looped, the stitching is done.
Bracing encircles the whole of the mount.

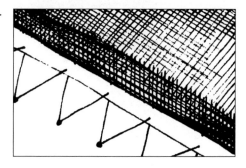

13 Trim off the surplus net, that is any net more than 3 holes away from the edge of the mount. Extreme caution must be exercised when cutting, because if the net is cut too close, the whole process must begin again.

14 Turn the edge under, so that it is trapped between the galloon and the top net. The edge of the net should line up with the edge of the galloon.

15 Sew the edge of the net with fine neat blanket stitching. This attaches the net to the galloon at the outer edge.

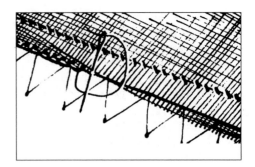

16 Press the stitching with hot pressing irons.

17 The positional springs are now made. See lesson twelve.
These are then sewn onto the foundation at the salient points, ie centre front, either one at centre front and then, two placed one either side of the parting or if there is no parting, then the three springs are placed to fan out at centre front. One spring is placed from earpeak to the inner edge of the mount (one at each side of the mount). One spring is placed from the temple peak to the inner edge of the mount (one at each side of the mount).

These last two springs cross on the galloon bind.

18 Press the springs, after stitching with heated pressing irons. It is best to press over tissue paper.

19 The tension elastics are now made and fixed, one at each end of the galloon bind. See lesson thirteen.

20 Refer to the workroom order form to check the way that the hair is required to fall.

21 Knot using single knotting (lesson ten), two rows every hole, every row around the outside of the mount. Knot the remainder of the mount as required by the order form.

22 If a parting is required, then it is made and inserted at this point in the proceedings.

23 Cut the bracing cotton.

24 Remove from the wooden block and turn inside out onto a malleable block.

25 Carry out at least two rows of underknotting, along the edge of the galloon.

26 Attach the hook and eye, one to each side of the galloon bind at centre back.

27 The semi transformation is then cut and dressed as required by the client.

Lesson Seventeen
Foundation postiche *The toupee*

A gentleman's toupee is a very intricate piece of postiche, as it is essential that it blends exactly with the wearer's own hair. The method of making is detailed in this section.

Tools and equipment required (Items with codes are available at Banbury Postiche Ltd)
Equipment used when measuring, and codes of these items are available at Banbury Postiche Ltd

Workroom order form complete
    with all details
Polythene template, as described
    in lesson four
Wooden block (MSMS2170)
Materials for shaping the wooden
    block if necessary, eg cotton wool
Galloon 5mm or 12mm (WG2481-2491)
Stiff foundation net or knotting
    Gauze (WN2550)
Oiled silk or similar commercial
    Material (WN2660)
Parting silk, if a drawn through
    parting is to be included
Lining , if required (WN2655)
Hammer (MS2290)

Block points (MS2280)
Pliers (MS2300)
White cotton
Sewing thread to match the hair
    colour (MS2210)
Needle (MS2330)
Thimble (MS2320)
Finger shield (MS2310)
Scissors (HS1550)
Positional springs (only if a drawn
    through parting is included)
Pressing irons
Tissue paper
Knotting holder and needle (KH2715-KH2740)
Malleable block (WB1700-1880)
T pins (HS1460)

It will take about one and a half hours to complete the theory of toupee making.

If this is a piece that you have decided to make as a sample, you can expect to spend several weeks on it.

The toupee
When considering the toupee, we have to understand the person for whom it is to be made.

What sort of man do you think he might be?
Some people think that a man who wears a toupee must be very vain.
This is not always the case. There are several reasons why a man decides to wear postiche.
It could be that he has lost his hair prematurely. The absence of hair can, in some instances, make a man look older than his years.
What problems could he encounter?
Below are the reasons that have been put forward to me.

1   Progression within his chosen career may be easier if he looks younger.

2   More confidence when attending interviews, particularly if against other younger men.

3   Makes the client feel younger when he is with his children.

4   Restoring confidence after hair loss due to an accident.

5   To cover scarring after surgery.

6   Restoring confidence where the hair loss has been caused by drugs.
    NB These could have been given by a doctor or self administered

and yes – you guessed it,

7   to make him more attractive to the other sex.

How does postiche for men differ from postiche for women?

First, the hair that is used must match exactly to the man's own hair. By this, I mean that if the man is 'greying' at the temples, then the toupee must also have a percentage of white hair included at the relevant points. The knotting for men's postiche is much finer. The fact that there is often very little hair to comb into the piece means that the choice of colour must be exact – nothing with which to disguise it.

The size of the toupee depends on the area to be covered.
If the man has an unusually shaped head, it may be beneficial to make a plaster cast of the head so that the finished toupee will be a perfect fit.

The attaching of a toupee also differs from feminine postiche in that there is no hair onto which to grip/pin the postiche. Several areas on the underside of the mount are covered with oiled silk, allowing the wearer to use toupee adhesive or toupee tape to fix the piece in position. These areas are called adhesive patches. Toupee adhesive is similar to spirit gum. Toupee tape is very fine double-sided tape. These adhesives have a remover with which to clean the scalp.

Where do you think the adhesive patches will be placed on the mount?

Check your answer.
Adhesive patches are placed at the points on the head where the toupee is most likely to pull away from the scalp.
Were you right?

Now you know about the toupee, we will progress to the actual making of one.

Method

1 Making reference to the workroom order form, make the pattern. The wooden block on which the toupee is to be made may require shaping if the client has any bumps etc. This will be on the work room order form. Often, all that is needed is some cotton wool or screwed up paper to be taped onto the block in the required position. If the client's head is very unusually shaped and a plaster cast has been made, then the cast is attached to the block. The main reason for a cast is if the client has had an accident which has left severe deformities.

2 Once you have the block correct, the hair must be obtained. It is not often that a toupee is made with one colour only. Mostly, the hair has to be mixed, to give an exact match. Some of the hair is mixed with white hair for the temples. One or more mixes may be needed for a gentleman's toupee.

3 Refer to the workroom order form to establish if the hair has to be precurled. If this is required it should be carried out at this point.

4 Mount the pattern onto the block.

5 Cross check the measurements with the workroom order form.

6 Point 5mm galloon around the outer edge of the pattern.

7 Outline the edges of the adhesive patches with the same galloon. The block points should face in towards the centre of the piece.

8 Outline the parting area, if there is one, with 5mm galloon.

9 If a lining is to be used, then it must be placed in position now.

10 Place stiff foundation net or knotting gauze over the top. Remove the points from underneath and replace with new ones on the top. The net may need to be moulded or pleated to make it fit the shape exactly. Sometimes a little moisture helps.

11 Sew the galloon to the net. The stitches must be very fine. Begin by sewing the inner edge of the adhesive patch areas.

Next, sew the inner edge of galloon which encircles the mount. This will take you all round the mount and both edges of the adhesive patch areas. The inner edge of the parting galloon is also stitched at this point.

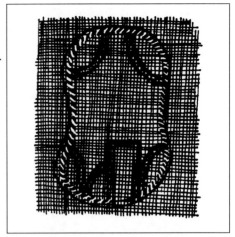

12 The mount must now be braced.
A running three point brace is the best method to use.

Brace the parting area.

13 Trim off the surplus net, that is, to within 3 holes of the galloon.

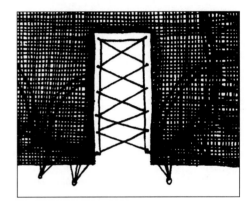

14 Fold the net under, so that it becomes trapped between the galloon and the top of the mount.

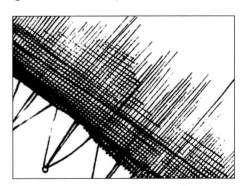

15 Using very fine blanket stitching, sew the net and galloon together. Do not sew the parting area.

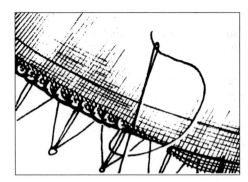

16 Press the stitching, using heated pressing irons.
The mount is now ready for knotting.
NB A toupee is frequently made using the edging without galloon (rolled edge) method.

Knotting a toupee

Traditionally, a toupee is knotted using single knotting, but reference must be made to the fact that commercially, double knotting with a single hair is now used – the reason being, that the knot is firmer for the process of blow drying.

1 Refer to the workroom order form, to see the direction that the mount is to be knotted.

2 Check on the workroom order form, the amount of hair required – that is, the density required.

3 Knot as directed. The usual pattern is to knot away from any parting.

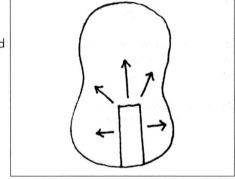

4 If a parting is to be included, then this is made and inserted at this point.

5 Cut the bracing cotton and remove the mount from the block.

6 Turn the mount upside down and fasten to a malleable block using T pins.

7 Underknot the outer edge of the galloon.
Follow the direction of the knotting on the top of the mount. At least two rows of underknotting are required.

The oiled silk is now sewn onto the base of the mount at the predetermined positions. Stitches must be very fine. Cut the silk to the correct size and shape, before sewing in position.

The toupee must then be cut and dressed. It is preferable if this can be done on the client, as the cut very much depends upon the way the client's own hair lies and the way the toupee blends with it.

Lesson Eighteen
Foundational postiche *The chignon*

The uses of and the method of making one of the most versatile pieces of added hair – the chignon – are explained in the following notes.

You will need the equipment that is listed below:
(Items with codes are available at Banbury Postiche Ltd)

Completed workroom order form
Pattern
Hammer (MS2290)
T pins (HS1460)
Wooden block (MS2170)
Needle (MS2330)
Galloon 12mm (WG2491)
Stiff foundation net (WN2550)
Positional springs

Block points (MS2280)
Pliers (MS2300)
White Cotton (MS2210)
Sewing thread to match the hair
colour (MS2210)
Hair (HF3100-3125)
Finger shield (MS2310)
Scissors (HS1550)
Malleable block (WB1700-1880)

To complete this theory section should take about three quarters to one hour. The revision section that follows will take approximately 20 minutes to complete.

If you decide to make a knotted chignon (a wise decision), it will take several weeks to complete. In this case I would suggest that you work through the theory, quickly, to begin with, then make the chignon, step by step with the notes. Finally, carry out the revision section at the end.

The chignon, pronounced sheen-yon, is one of the most versatile of hairpieces.

Do you know anything of the chignon?

What do you understand when the word chignon is mentioned?

Most people, when asked that question, understand the chignon to
be a bun worn at the nape of the neck. Is that what you thought?

Well, if it is, you are partly right.
The truth is that the term chignon can be used – indeed, is used – in certain circles, for any piece of added hair that is not a complete wig.

This can be confusing.

The most important chignon, is the knotted chignon.
This piece of postiche is usually made of short, curled hair and worn on the crown, to give added height to the dressing, or in the nape, to give extra length to the dressing hiding the short hair at the nape in certain styles.

In addition a chignon can mean:

a coil of hair worn on the crown or down the back

a cluster of curls worn at the nape or on the back of the head

a plaited hairpiece worn on the crown, or again, down the back of the head.

That may seem to be quite a number of uses for one hairpiece.
The reason is that more than one type of postiche is called a chignon, when used in one of the ways mentioned above.

Let me explain further.

The diamond mesh	This may be worn on the crown, a chignon
The marteau	When worn in the nape, termed a chignon
The switch	Coiled or plaited and worn on the crown or down the back, becomes a chignon

See if you can think of the definition of a chignon.

I wonder if your definition is similar to mine.
A chignon is a piece of postiche, usually made of short, curled hair which is worn either in the nape or on the crown.

How close were you?

How is a knotted chignon made?
Like most foundational postiche, the knotted chignon is made on a base of net, with the hair being knotted onto the net in the direction of the -?-.

Method

1   Read your workroom order form.
     Check that you know what is required.

2   Take the pattern. If you have forgotten how to make the pattern, re-read lesson seven.

3   Using as few block points as possible, point the pattern into position on the block.

What position would that be?

4   5mm galloon is now used to outline the edge of the pattern.

5   Sew where the two edges meet, with small neat stitches.

6   Check with your workroom order form if a lining is to be used. If it is, it is placed into position now. NB Take the points out from underneath as you progress.

7   Point stiff foundation net over the pattern, galloon and lining (if used). The net may require pleating or moulding to gain an exact shape.

Did you remember to remove the points from underneath as you progressed?

Good.

8   Sew the inner edge of the outlining galloon to the net with cotton -?-.
Very fine hemming stitches are used.

9   Can you remember how to brace a mount?

Explain briefly how to brace your mount using running brace.
If you are unsure of this process, then check up with lesson eleven.

10 Once your mount has been braced, you can remove the block points which have been holding the mount.

11 The net which extends more than three holes further than the edge of the galloon, can now be trimmed off.

12 This raw edge of net is then turned under and trapped between the galloon and upper edge of net.

13 Stitch the two edges together, using very fine blanket stitches.

14 Finally, press the stitching, using a heated pressing iron. Next, the positional springs are made and inserted. These are explained in lesson twelve. It might be beneficial to revise this area at this point.

15 Sew the positional springs into position. If the chignon is to be worn on the crown, then the springs are placed crossing at the centre.

If the mount is for the nape the springs are placed at either side.

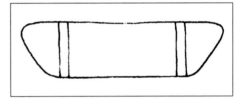

16 The next stage is to knot the mount.
Refer to the workroom order form for details of the direction the hair is required to fall.
Single knotting is used.

17 When the whole of the top has been knotted, the mount is removed from the wooden block.

18 Underknotting is the next and final stage of knotting. Turn the mount inside out and attach to a -?- block using T pins. At least two rows of underknotting are needed on the edge of the galloon.

19 One of three methods of attaching the chignon to the head is used:

Using a cache peigne (hidden comb)   Stitch into position

With two loops   Six threads of cotton covered with blanket stitches at each end

With hairgrips   Gripped to the client's own hair

20 The knotted chignon is complete.

It is advisable to carry out a preliminary dressing on the chignon. Using T pins, fix the chignon the correct way up and in its intended position, onto the malleable block. The chignon can now be styled as directed on the workroom order form.

Revision test

The Chignon

Without referring back to the text or to your notes, answer the following on a separate sheet:

1   How would you write the word chignon phonetically, the way it is spoken?

2   What type of hair is most generally used?

3   List two other pieces of postiche which can be worn and called a chignon.

4   What are the two main reasons for wearing a chignon?

5   What is the main selling point of a chignon?

6   Where is the pattern placed on the wooden block?

7   What size of galloon is used?

8   Where is the galloon used?

9   What type of net is used?

10   What other material may be required at this point?

11   Where would we find this information?

12   What is bracing?

13   What type of bracing is used?

14   How many positional springs are used?

15   Where are they positioned...

a   on a chignon for the crown?

b   on a chignon for the nape?

16   When, why and how is a malleable block used?

17   Give the three methods of attaching the chignon to the head.

Lesson Nineteen
Foundational postiche *The fringe*

In this section, I shall explain the measuring and making of a piece of postiche which covers the fringe area. In this lesson you will learn how to edge a piece of postiche without using galloon.

Equipment used when measuring, and codes of these items which are available at Banbury Postiche Ltd

Equipment needed

Tape measure (MS2360)
Paper for pattern
Eyebrow pencil
Workroom order form
Pencil
Scissors (HS1550)
Sellotape
Galloon (WG2491-2481)
Stiff foundation net (WN2550)
Cotton to match hair colour
White cotton (MS2210)
Wooden block (MS2170)

Malleable block (WB1700-1880)
Block points (MS2280)
Hammer (MS2290)
Pliers (MS2300)
Positional springs (from 1 to 3
    depending on the size and shape)
Two tension elastics
Hook and eye
Hair of the required colour (HF3100-3125)
Knotting needle and holder (KH2715-KH2740)
Drawing mats (DM2880)
Pressing irons

Reading through the theory section should take approximately 45 minutes.

Follow this by thirty minutes on the revision section.

The fringe

As its name suggests, this piece of postiche is worn at the front area of the head, where a fringe would be worn. For this reason it is occasionally called a front. It is usually quite a small piece – average size 15cm long and 4 to 8cms in depth.

Why would a fringe be worn?

Where the client has a receding hairline.
Where the hair is too fine to have any style formation.
After accident or illness where treatment has caused hairloss.
After accident or operation which has left scarring or an unsightly hairline.
To give fashion effects, for example, different colours without the effect being permanent.

Making the pattern

1   Prepare pattern making equipment.

2   Discuss the requirements of the client. Establish the reasons for wanting this type of postiche.

3   Fill in the client's name, address etc on the workroom order form.

Write in the requirements of the client – the style with which it is to blend in. All other details should be filled in as they are taken.

4   Measure the area to be covered.

a   If there is no hairline evident, then refer to a past photograph.

b   In most cases, the hairline can be judged by the fine hair that remains.

c   Draw the hairline you are to work to, onto the client's scalp, using an eyebrow pencil.

Obviously, if the piece is for fashion use, there will be no need for this procedure.

d   Measure from the centre front, straight back to the furthermost point that the piece is required.

e   Measure across at intervals. The number of these depends on the depth required for the final mount.

f   The circumference measurement will also be needed.

5   Make sure that you transfer these measurements to your workroom order form.

6   Next, mark the measurements onto the paper for the pattern.

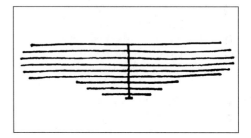

7   Draw in the hairline.

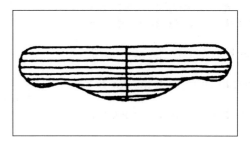

8   Cut out the pattern.

9   Try the pattern in position on the client. It may help to moisten it slightly.

10 Strengthen the edges with sellotape.

11 If you are satisfied with the shape of the pattern, point it on a wooden block, in the position it will be worn. Point at centre front and at the opposite point at the back of the pattern.
Then point at each end of the pattern.

12 Point 1cm galloon around the circumference of the block. Begin at centre back. Leave l0cms etc on each end, at the centre back for the tension elastics.

13 Take a rectangle of stiff foundation net, slightly larger than the fringe area to be covered.

14 Find the centre of the net and point it at the centre of the pattern.
Remove the block points from the galloon bind as you work outwards, replacing as you go.

15 Sew either side of the galloon bind in very fine hemming stitches.

16 The mount is now edged without galloon.

Following the edge of the pattern, sew in small
running stitches. As you progress, pull gently on the
sewing silk so that the net gathers a little and hugs the block.

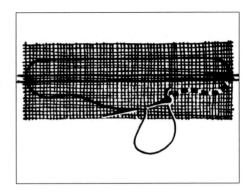

17 Trim the surplus net – that is, any net which extends over
one and a half centimetres.

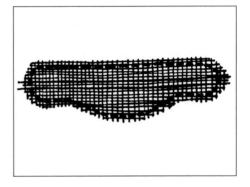

18 The mount is braced next.
The bracing stitches are made into the running stitches
that follow the pattern. A running three point brace is
the best method to use.

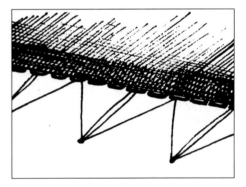

19 Fold the net over and tuck the raw edge in.

20 Sew in fine hemming stitches.

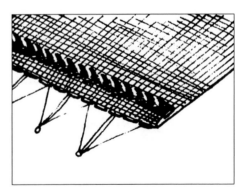

21 Press all the stitching.

22 The positional springs are made and sewn into position at this point.

a If the widest part is to the rear of the fringe then it is usual to place a spring at the centre front.

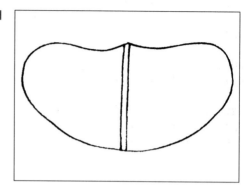

b If the fringe is to include a parting then a spring is placed on either side of the parting.

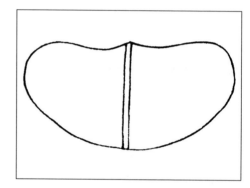

c Where the fringe follows the hairline as far as the temple peaks, then three springs are used – one at centre front and the other two, one each side from temple peak, sloping in to the rear of the mount.

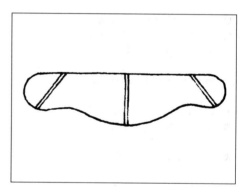

23 Press the stitching.

24 The mount is now ready for knotting. Can you remember which type of knot to use, if a very short and fine result is required?

Just in case you could not remember, it is point knotting that is used for this result.

Knotting

Place the hair to be knotted, into the drawing brushes. If point knotting, the hair is placed into the drawing brushes with the points protruding.
Using a fine needle, commence by knotting the extreme edge in fine point knotting. It is preferable to under draw these knots, completely enclosing the edge. Continue to knot the mount, working in the direction indicated by the workroom order form. Normally, this is away from the centre front or the parting, if one is included.

After the net has been completely knotted, cut the bracing cotton and remove from the wooden block.

Turn upside down and pin on a malleable block, using T pins. Carry out two rows of underknotting. Next, make the tension elastics. These are made, one at each end of the galloon bind. If you remember, it was left 10cms longer at each end for this purpose. The tension elastic should draw the galloon up so that the length of the mount from galloon end, to galloon end, is the same as the circumference.

Finally, sew a hook and eye at the centre back. The hook should be sewn to face away from the scalp. The fringe is now made. Refer to the workroom order form, to establish the way it must be dressed. Style and dress accordingly.

Revision test

The fringe

Without referring back to the text or to your notes, answer the following on a separate sheet.

1   What is the other name for a fringe?
2   Why is this?
3   How is the fringe attached to the head?
4   When edging without galloon, what stitching follows the edge of the pattern?
5   Briefly, explain edging without galloon.
6   Where are positional springs placed?
7   Where are the tension elastics placed?
8   What type of knotting is used for a fringe?
9   Give three reasons why a fringe might be worn.
10 What is the use of the galloon bind?

Lesson Twenty
Foundational postiche *Facial postiche*

The making of facial postiche, that is beards and moustaches, is explained in this lesson.
Also, we consider the reasons for their use.

Tools and equipment required (Items with codes are available at Banbury Postiche Ltd)

Completed workroom order form
Pattern
Chin block or malleable block (WB1700-WB1900)
Chinagraph pencil
Transparent tape

Hair lace (WN2625)
Block points (MS2280)
Nylon thread (MS2042)
Yak hair (HF3160)
Knotting holder and fine knotting needle
(K2715-KH2740)

Allow yourself approximately thirty minutes to work your way through the theory section.

Follow this by filling in the gaps in the revision passage that follows.
For this you should allow fifteen minutes.

Facial postiche

When do you think facial postiche might be used?
Read on and see if your answers coincided with mine.

Facial postiche is an integral part of actors' wardrobes. This is quite obvious, as they must be able to
play many different parts, requiring different looks.

Facial postiche is also used for disguise. I am not speaking here of the types of disguise beards etc sold
for children's playwear, although they can form part of the wigmaker's work. The type of facial postiche
I am referring to is that which is used by 'spies'. To disguise themselves the postiche they wear, must be
perfectly natural.

There is one other major reason for the wearing of facial postiche. The people involved, are those who
have suffered accident or injury to their faces and are disfigured. They can gain a tremendous amount of
confidence if their disfigurement can be covered by natural-looking facial postiche. This group of clients
is from the male population.

Thinking about the foundational postiche we have already covered, you will be able to understand that
facial postiche needs yet another method of production. Foundation edged with galloon would most
definitely be too thick. Foundation edged without galloon would also be too thick.
So what are we to do?

First of all, we use a material called hair lace. This is exactly what it sounds – single lengths of hair, laced
together – one reason good facial postiche is very expensive. Second, there is no edging carried out.
The knotting is done on the hair lace and a raw edge is left for the client to stick to the skin and blend in
as necessary.

Facial postiche
The beard

Method

1   Prepare all equipment.

2   Refer to the workroom order form for the measurements required.

3   Refer to the pattern to establish the growth pattern required.

4   Using a chinagraph pencil, draw the shape of the required beard onto the chin block
    or point pattern in position.

5   Mark growth lines across the chin and cheek.

6   Next, indicate the growth pattern required for the finished postiche.

7   Cover with transparent tape, the lines which you have drawn. This helps to avoid marking the hair lace.

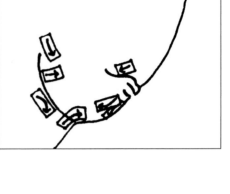

8   Take a piece of hair lace large enough to cover the area.

9   Hold the net so that the holes are straight up and down.

10 Stretch the hair lace over the chin block.

11 Point at CF above the pattern indicated on the block.

12 Point below the pattern, under the chin, at a point directly beneath the top point.

13 Making certain that the hair lace is lying flat, place a block point at each side, just beyond the pattern.

14 Block points are now placed around the outside of the pattern, leaving a minimum of 25mm of hair lace between the edge of the pattern and the points.

15 The hair lace is now held unevenly in position.

16 About six pleats will be needed to shape the lace to fit the chin. These are made and pointed. It is advisable to alternate the direction of each pleat.

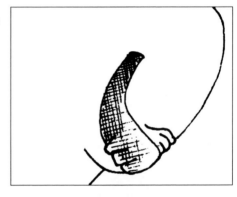

17 Take a length of nylon thread and starting at one end, carry out a double knot with the end of the thread.

18 Whip the pleats together. The thread passes through one hole and on to the next.

19 Try to use the same length of thread for all the stitching.

20 Finish with a double knot.

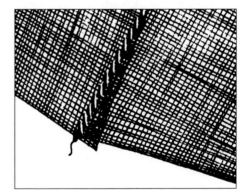

21 Refer to your workroom order form, to check the density required for the finished postiche.

22 Knot the beard, as required in very fine single knotting.
   NB The knots are made in the opposite direction so that the beard is given natural lift and texture.

23 You have now completed your beard.

The moustache

Method

1 Prepare all equipment.
2 Refer to workroom order form for details of finished postiche.
3 Take pattern which has been made previously or make a pattern to the measurements given.
4 The pattern is then taped onto a malleable block.
5 Take a piece of hair lace and stretch it over the pattern.
6 Point in position, ensuring that there is a gap of 25mm all around the pattern.
7 Knot the moustache.

NB The postiche is knotted at an off angle which will make the hair lie in towards the centre and in the opposite direction. This will cause a natural lift and texture to form

8 You have now made a moustache.

Finishing facial postiche

The beard or moustache must now be gently combed into the desired direction, taking care not to disturb the natural lift you have created. All that remains is for the postiche to be shaped. Wherever possible the cutting of facial postiche is best carried out on the client.

Revision test

Beards and moustaches

Without referring to your notes or back to the text, answer the following on a separate sheet.

Beards and moustaches are called -?-.

There are several reasons why they might be worn.
They are -?-.

The measurements for the beard are transferred to the -?- using
a -?- pencil.

These markings are covered with -?- to stop -?-.

The material used for the foundation is called -?-.

When pointing the material into position, it is essential to leave -?- around the outer edge of the -?-.
Where pleating is required, this must be -?- together,
using a single length of -?-.

The stitching for the pleats begins and ends with a -?-.
When making a moustache, the pattern is taped onto a -?-.

Knotting of facial postiche is carried out -?- to give natural -?-.

Wherever possible, facial postiche should be -?- on the client.

Lesson Twenty One
Partings

In this section will be explained the two main methods of making a parting – the English method and the French method.

Equipment required (Items with codes are available at Banbury Postiche Ltd)

Malleable block (WB1700-1880)
Drawing mats (DM2880)
Knotting needle and holder (KH2740-KH2715)
Knotting gauze
Scissors (HS1550)

T pins (HS1460)
Hair to be knotted (HF3100-3125)
Stiff foundation net (WN2550)
Parting silk
Coloured paper for pattern

Partings

The most successful partings are made separately and then inserted into the finished mount.

We have previously talked about the knotted parting, using directional knotting.
The disadvantage with this method is that the net may be seen.

With the other methods, the hair is drawn through a piece of flesh coloured silk, which then resembles the scalp.

The English method

1   Draw out a pattern onto a piece of paper. It is best if this paper is of a colour which allows the net to be seen more easily.

2   Pin the pattern onto the malleable block.

3   Pin a piece of fine net or knotting gauze over the top.

4   Knot in very fine, single knotting.
    Stiff foundation net – every hole, every row.
    Knotting gauze – every other hole, every other row.
    Start your knotting 2cms in from the front edge
    of the pattern.

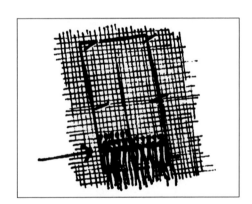

5   As each row of knots is completed, the roots are cut away as close as possible to the knot.

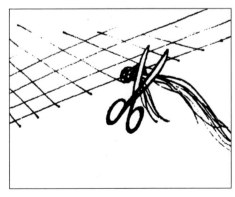

6   Knot the final three rows of knotting thicker than the rest. This makes the parting thicker at its end.

7   Cover the whole of the pattern area, except for the front 2cms.

Now the knotting is completed and all the roots have been cut, we proceed to the drawing through stage.

1   Comb the hair towards the front of the parting.

2   To smooth some coating conditioner on the hair, helps at this stage. Only use a small amount, though.

3   Firmly pin a piece of flesh-coloured parting silk over the top of the knotting.

4   Fix a fine gauze hook into the knotting needle holder. This is similar to a knotting needle.

5   Begin at the back of the parting, where the hair should be drawn through thicker than the rest of the parting.

6   The hook is inserted through the gauze. It is preferable for the hook to be at right angles to the net.

7   Two or three hairs only are pulled through, each time the hook goes in.

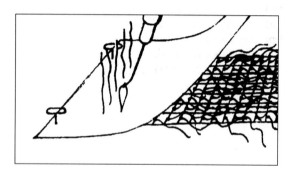

8   Complete one row at a time.
     The spacing should be as close to the knotting spaces as is possible.

9   You will find that, although you did not knot the front 2cms, there will be ample hair to be drawn through.

As you develop your techniques, you will find that you are able to insert your hook several times before pulling the hair through to its ends. A distance between 1 and 2cms can be covered.

It always gives a finer finish if the last two rows to be drawn through, that is the two at the front hairline, are drawn much finer and closer together.

After knotting and drawing through, remove the T pins that have been holding it onto the malleable block. Take the parting off the block and trim off the excess hair. Next, trim the net on which you knotted, so that it is quite close to the edge of the knotting. Turn under the parting silk and hem, in extremely fine hemming stitches. The parting is now ready to be positioned into the final postiche. Using as few block points as possible, pin the parting into position. Neatly sew down both sides and across the back, in fine running stitches. Remove the block points. Lastly, it may require one or two knots, to fill in any gaps that might show.

Partings

The French method

This method differs from the English, in that both the knotting and the drawing through are done together. This may sound easier, but I would suggest that you practice the English method first.

Method

1 Onto the malleable block, pin the pattern, the net or gauze and the parting silk.

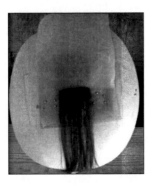

2 The parting silk is pinned at the front edge only.

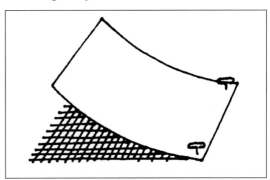

3 Insert a fine knotting needle through the parting silk and knot into the net/gauze below. The silk is transparent enough for the net to be seen through at this point.

4 After the knot has been carried out securely, the hair is drawn through the silk.

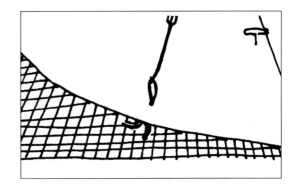

To summaries

Insert the needle through the silk, knot into the net and draw through all layers.

Continue in this way, until all the partings area has been knotted. As you work away from the front, it is best to pin the silk firmly, every centimetre or so. Knot the back of the parting more closely together, to give a thicker result.

Again, after the knotting and drawing through has been completed, the net is trimmed close to the knotting. Then the parting silk is turned under and hemmed. The parting is now inserted into the waiting postiche, as described earlier.

Lesson Twenty Two
Cleaning postiche
This lesson covers the different methods of cleaning postiche and the equipment used.

Tools and materials used (Items with codes are available at Banbury Postiche Ltd)

Block holder (BH1330)
Malleable block (WB1700-1880)
T pins (HS1460)
Bowl

Water
Shampoo (TA1092)or (HS4001)
Brushes and combs
Protective gloves

The theoretical section should take about thirty minutes to complete. Follow this, by cleansing postiche – step by step, with the notes.

After completion, answer the revision test that follows the text. Allow approximately 20 minutes.

Cleaning postiche

The cleansing and dressing of postiche can be a valuable asset to a salon. This type of work can be carried out at the beginning of the week when the salon is likely to be quiet. It will keep qualified operatives busy all week – good for them and for your business.

Before beginning to clean any postiche, you must establish the type of hair from which the piece has been made.

What different types of hair do you know?

Basically, there are two different types of hair when we are considering the cleansing of postiche.
They are:
Artificial hair
Human or animal hair

Each type of hair is cleaned in a different way.

The way that the postiche is made, is also a consideration. It may be a woven piece or it could be knotted onto a net or stretch base.

Frequently, there is an area of the salon which is set aside for the cleansing and dressing of postiche.

Due to Health and Safety Laws cleaning of a real hair pastiche with cleaning fluid needs to be carried out by a specialized company with the correct cleaning machine. Banbury Postiche Ltd is one such company who provide this service.

Equipment for a wig boutique

Malleable blocks of varying Sizes	Used to hold the foundation whilst working. Must be stored in a dry place.
The block holder	To hold the malleable block.
Postiche pins	Shaped like a T. Used to pin the foundation onto the block. These must be stored carefully.
Brushes & combs	Keep clean and sterile.

Shampoos- (HS4001) For synthetic hair products and (TA1092) for Real Hair

Water	
Bowl	
Protective gloves	To prevent the hands from drying.
Towels	These are used to remove excess water. Keep clean.
Pinching irons	Used in the curling of postiche.
Heater	For irons.
Tissue paper	For 'en papillotte'.
Rollers, clips etc	For setting postiche.
Tape	For waving postiche.
Scissors	For styling postiche.
Hand dryer	For blowdrying the hair.

When a client brings a piece of postiche into the salon there are certain procedures which must be done before it can be cleaned. As we have already stated, the first thing that must be established is the type of hair. We can now prepare the equipment and materials according to the type of hair. Next, we must examine the foundation to see if it requires mending.

Repairing the foundation

Fault	Remedy
Worn tension elastic	Replace with a new tension elastic
Worn positional springs	Replace with new springs
Small hole	Darn and knot over
Large hole	Sew in a piece of net then reknot over the area.

A piece of postiche which has been bought 'off the shelf' may require adjusting.

Fault	Remedy
Up to 2cms too big	Tighten the tension elastic
More than 2cms too big	Make a small tuck at CB or two small tucks one at either side of the nape.
A little too tight	Loosen tension elastic
Very tight	Insert a small amount of net at CB or two pieces, one at either side of the nape. Then knot over the new net.

When any necessary repairs have been made, the postiche can be cleaned.

Select the method of cleaning.

Cleaning human and animal hair

Please consult a professional cleaning company such as Banbury Postiche Ltd, where the product will be returned ready to be styled.

Where the hair is in a poor condition or in a very dry state, it should be treated with a wax conditioner. The wax must be rinsed thoroughly but care should be taken not to wet the base more than is absolutely necessary.

Cleaning artificial hair

Artificial hair is made from synthetic fibres.

1 Prepare a bowl of lukewarm water with shampoo.
2 Turn the postiche inside out.
3 Place the postiche into the water and allow to penetrate.
4 Squeeze the postiche, gently, to allow the dirt to be removed.
5 Transfer to a bowl containing clear water.
6 Rinse the postiche free from shampoo.
7 Gently squeeze out the excess moisture.
8 Allow the postiche to dry naturally.
9 Attach the postiche to a malleable block.
10 Brush the postiche into the desired shape.

At this point, I would like to mention a method of cleaning human hair wigs which is not, at this present time, part of any scheme. It is a commercial method which defies all the standard rules.
Please remember that!!!

A malleable block is completely covered with polythene.
The wig is then fixed firmly in position on the block, using T pins.

A strong solution of green soft soap or similar and water is made in a jug.

A sponge is immersed into the solution and drawn along the hair, in sections, from roots to points.

When all the hair has been 'washed' the wig, on its block is placed under a spray and the solution rinsed away. The water must run from roots to points.

A towel is then placed over the wig and the surplus moisture removed by gentle pressing.

The postiche can then be set & dressed as required. Because the wig has been held in shape and at the right size, the foundation has not been allowed to shrink.
NB This service is also available at Banbury Postiche Ltd.

Practical application

It would be helpful to you at this point to take three pieces of postiche and clean them, using a different method for each.

Write up your findings, stating which you prefer and why.

Cleaning postiche

On a separate sheet, answer the following questions, without referring back to your notes or to the text.

1 Why is it necessary to clean postiche?
2 Which type of postiche can always be cleaned in soap and water?
3 What must be done before any cleaning can take place?
4 How would you correct a wig which had become too loose?
5 Name the springs which might need replacing.
6 How would you mend a wig that had become torn?
7 If the hair is in a dry and poor state, what would you use to counteract it?
8 How are the hands protected?
9 What would happen if the base was allowed to become saturated, when conditioning postiche?

Lesson Twenty Three
The cutting of postiche
I will explain to you in this section the most advisable methods of cutting postiche.

The following equipment would be required if you were to carry out the cutting of postiche

Equipment used when measuring (Items with codes are available at Banbury Postiche Ltd)

Workroom order form
Malleable block (MS1700-1880)
T pins (HS1460)
Block holder (BH1330)
Gowns (HS1562) etc for client protection
Combs (Black Diamond range)

Brushes
Scissors (SC1250) – for cutting hair
Razor (SC1100)
Neck brush
Water spray (HS1578)
Back mirror

I would suggest that you allow yourself forty five minutes to work through the text.

Cutting postiche

Can you think of three reasons for cutting postiche?

What methods of cutting do you think would be used?

Do you think the method of cutting postiche differs from the method of cutting a head of hair?

All right.
Did you think I was just going to ask you questions in this section and not give out any information?

No! I wanted you to begin to think about postiche itself without being prompted or
answered immediately.

The answers are in the following text.
Check your answers against the text as it progresses.

Having made several pieces of postiche already, you will understand that once a piece has been made,
it has rather rough edges.
These must be trimmed and shaped to give the correct effect.
Therefore, one reason for cutting postiche is to create shape and form.

Another reason that you may need to cut postiche, is to reduce
length and bulk.
This is needed to give a good foundation on which to work.

When a piece of postiche is made, it is made to a workroom order form.
The shape will be cut initially to the description or photograph. When the client is fitted with the pos-
tiche, he/she may want further alterations.
So, shall we now itemise the reasons for cutting postiche?

1   To produce style formation, ie shape and form.
2   To reduce the length and/or bulk of a piece, to give a good base.
3   To achieve the style/shape requested on the workroom order form.
4   To rearrange the style formation, in order to please the client.

Postiche can be cut wet or dry.

Methods of cutting postiche

Postiche that has been dampened using a water spray, may be cut by the following methods:
Club cutting using the scissors
Tapering using the razor

Postiche may be cut dry, using one or more of the methods that follow:

Club cutting
Tapering
Point cutting   Using the scissors
Thinning

Any other method of cutting, or combination of cutting techniques, may be employed to achieve the desired result. What does one have to consider, when cutting postiche?

First of all, there is the way in which the postiche has been made.

If the piece is weft made, then the cutting will have to be modified.
This is to allow for the fact that most weft made postiche has areas which appear thicker than others, until they are dressed. It is preferable in this case to dress the postiche in the desired style and then cut away the excess. Where a piece has a foundational base, the finished result is more even and therefore more natural. The cutting can proceed almost exactly as if the hair were attached to a client.

Second, you must consider the amount of hair.

It could be that a foundation has been knotted thicker in some areas. Your approach to this problem should be exactly the same as it would be on any head of hair. More tapering would be done in this area to balance the style – that is, unless there was a reason for the bulk, for example at the rear of a parting.

As with any haircut, consideration must be given to the client him/herself.

The client's build and height affect the choice of style.
The facial characteristics determine the outer perimeter shape.
Before any cutting takes place, the personality and lifestyle of the client requires consideration.

It is important to note any abnormalities that might be present.
These are almost always present after accidents.
If the client has an indented scalp, then the hair in this area should be left longer so that the style can be built up giving a symmetrical finish.

Method

1   Gown the client to protect their clothes from falling hair.

2   Fix the postiche to the client's head.
    Alternatively the postiche may be pinned onto a malleable block.

3   Check the workroom order form for the style required.
    Remember to take into consideration the points listed earlier.

Which points can you remember?

4   Decide which method or combination of methods of cutting you are going to use.

5   Arrange onto your trolley the tools required.

6   Section the hair according to the cut to be carried out.

7   Proceed with the cut, as normal.
    This normally begins with the cutting of the base line.
    Cutting lines and angles are then used to produce the desired effect.

8   On completing the cut, check over from every angle.

9   Using a neck brush, remove all the hair that may have dropped onto the shoulders of the client.

10 Using a back mirror, show the client the finished result.
    If he/she is satisfied, then proceed with the setting or blowdrying, as required on
    the workroom order form.

Precautions when cutting
a   Always cover the client's clothing.
b   Always refer to the workroom order form.
c   Make appropriate partings.
d   Choose the correct tools for the job.
e   Do not use a mirror if the client is sceptical (eg after accident).
f   Keep all guards on razors etc.
g   Use the neck brush frequently.
h   Use an autoclave, glass bead sterilizer or boiler for scissors etc.

Faults	How to avoid them
An unbalanced style	Refer to workroom order form
	Choose your tools correctly
	Take care choosing the techniques
	Make clean partings
	Sections should follow style
	Control cutting angles
	Use a mirror if appropriate
Cutting too short	Refer to workroom order form
	Ensure you understand the client's requirements
	Control your tools carefully
	Choose the correct technique
Tangling of roots & points	Only taper the hair shorter than 7cms unless the hair has been point knotted with the roots cut down to 1cm.
Damaging the foundation	Do not over wet the base
	Take care when sectioning
	Use your tools with care
	Do not tug when using scissors/razor

Lesson Twenty Four
Setting and dressing postiche
This lesson takes you one step closer to the completion of the postiche.
You will learn different ways of setting the hair and how to dress the postiche.

Tools and equipment required (Items with codes are available at Banbury Postiche Ltd)

Workroom order form
Block holder (BH1330)
Malleable block (WB1700-1880)
T pins (HS1460)
Combs (BD comb range)
Brushes (Denman Range)
Jug
Water
Setting lotions/sprays
Rollers & pins (HS1590-1670)
Clips (PC2091)

Neutralising rinse
Dressing cream
Hair net (DH1597)
Tape (TAPEW)
Postiche oven
Hood dryer
Hand dryer
Tissue paper
Hair spray
Wig box/case

Allow yourself about 30 minutes to work through the theory aspect.
Follow that by a period applying the theory in practice.
Finally, work through the revision section.

Setting and dressing postiche
After the postiche has been made, it requires styling to the client's requirements.
These are noted on the workroom order form.
If the wig is for a client who has lost hair through accident or injury and the intention is to create the same look as he/she had previously, then there is often a photograph to follow.

Wherever possible, carry out any cutting that may be needed, on the client.

A workroom order form should be completed, even if the postiche has only been brought to the salon for cleaning and dressing. This way, the object of setting and dressing postiche, that of achieving a style requested by the client, may be carried out fully. Note carefully the amount of curl or wave required.

Look for the style direction.
It can be disastrous to style a wig to the wrong side, particularly where the client is still in a state of shock.

Equipment

Workroom order form	Contains all the details of the style.
Block holder	Clamps onto the table, holds the malleable block.
Malleable block	Canvas covered block stuffed with sawdust. Holds the postiche during preparation.
T pins (postiche pins)	Used to secure the postiche to the malleable block.
Jug and water	Used when damping the hair before setting.
Combs & brushes	Must be kept clean and sterile.

	Used as appropriate to the style.
Rollers, pins & clips	Must be kept clean and sterile. Used as appropriate to the style.
Setting lotion/spray	Helps the style to stay for a longer period. Can help in controlling the hair.
Neutralising rinse	A coloured rinse which is used to eliminate yellow discolouration from white hair.
Net	Used to cover the hair in pli whilst drying.
Tape	If the postiche is to be set in waves, then this is carried out using a fabric tape and postiche pins.
Postiche oven	Used for drying the postiche. Choice of equipment is dependent on style required.
Hood dryer	Check the plugs and cables before each use.
Hand dryer	Equipment should be in good working order.
Tissue paper	When drying white postiche, it is covered with tissue paper to prevent yellow discolouration.
Dressing cream	Used for control, where there is static electricity.
Hair spray	A non-shellac product must be used. This helps the style to stay.
Wig box/case	For storing the postiche.

You may ask whether the setting of postiche is any different from setting normally.
The answer is that there are precautions that must be taken but any technique that is used in a salon can be used in the setting of postiche.

Precautions when setting postiche
The correct size of malleable block must be used.
The postiche must be secured to the block in the correct position.
The postiche must be secured firmly to the block, using postiche pins.
Take great care when wetting the hair, that the net foundation does not become saturated.
Do not allow the roller pins to rip at the foundation.
Use a cool to warm dryer only to prevent discolouration.
Do not disturb the knots when brushing and combing the hair.

Roller setting postiche

1   Check the style required with the workroom order form or the client's record card.

2   Choose the correct size of malleable block.

3   Choose the correct size of rollers for the desired style.

4   Pin the postiche onto the block in the position it will be worn.

5   Dip a comb into a jug of warm water and shake the water onto the hair to dampen it. Take care not to saturate the base.

6   If working on white hair, it might be necessary to apply a neutralising rinse at this point.

7   Take clean neat sections, avoiding pulling at the knots.

8   Set in the required style.

9   Secure the rollers without pulling the foundation and causing distortion. Avoid damage to the foundation, by placing the roller pins into the roller in front, rather than onto the base. Avoid marking the hair.

10 Cover the block with a net.

11 If working on white hair, then it is advisable to cover with tissue paper to prevent discolouration.

12 Dry the postiche, either in a postiche oven or under a warm hood drier. If working with white hair, then the oven or drier must be set to cool. White hair can also be left to dry naturally.

13 After drying, allow the postiche to cool before removing the rollers etc.

Dressing the postiche
After the hair has been allowed to cool and the rollers have been very carefully removed, the hair is brushed through to remove the roller marks etc. Brushing should be carried out with great care, so that the knots are not disturbed. A soft bristle brush is advised. Next, brush the hair into the style stated on the workroom order form or record card. A dressing cream may be used if there is a lot of static. Place a small amount into the palm of the hand and spread between the palms before stroking through the hair. Back combing and back brushing may be used if necessary. Use any techniques required to produce the final dressing. Spray lightly with hair spray to help to keep the style in position. A non-shellac base for the spray is essential to avoid a heavy build up.

Removing the postiche from the block
Carefully remove the postiche pins that have been holding the postiche in position on the malleable block. The postiche can now be gently removed from the block. Pad the inside with tissue paper to keep its shape. Place the postiche into a wig box/case which has been lined with tissue paper and store until required. Alternatively, the postiche can be stored on the malleable block.

Blow drying postiche
Great care must be taken when blow drying the hair, not to disturb the knots.
Each section should be taken, before placing onto the brush, so that the bristles do not tug and loosen the knots. Consult the workroom order form/record card to establish the style required.
Choose the right size of malleable block. Prepare the brushes and combs etc that are needed.
Secure the postiche in position on the malleable block using postiche pins.
Dampen the hair by shaking water from a comb which has been dipped into a jug of warm water.
If working with white hair, it might be necessary to use a neutralising rinse. Take clean neat sections, starting at the base of the style and blow dry as required.
Do not tug at the meshes of hair, as this could result in distortion of the foundation.

Dressing the postiche
Allow the hair to cool before dressing. Once again, brushing should be carried out with great care so that the knots are not disturbed. A soft bristle brush is advised. Check the style required on the workroom order form or record card. A dressing cream may be used if there is a lot of static.
Place a small amount into the palm of the hand and spread between the palms before stroking through the hair. Back combing and back brushing may be used if necessary. Use any techniques required to produce the final dressing. Spray lightly with hair spray to help to keep the style in position.

A non-shellac base for the spray is essential to avoid a heavy build up. Carefully remove the postiche pins that have been holding the postiche in position on the malleable block.
The postiche can now be removed from the block. Pad the inside with tissue paper to keep its shape. Place the postiche into a wig box/case which has been lined with tissue paper and store until required. Alternatively the postiche can be stored on the malleable block.

Setting postiche into waves

Waves can be formed at the back of the wig, by placing rollers vertically across that section. The nape area is usually set to brush upwards. Secure the wig onto a malleable block of the correct size, using postiche pins. Dampen the hair by shaking water from a comb which has been dipped into a jug of warm water. Comb through from roots to points taking care not to pull at the knots. Refer to the workroom order form/record card for the style requirements. Sectioning the hair with great care, place the rollers into the top section of the wig to the desired style. The back section is set as shown in the diagram opposite.

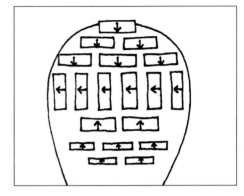

Using reverse pincurling to produce soft waves over the whole of the head

Secure the wig onto a malleable block of the correct size, using postiche pins. Dampen the hair by shaking water from a comb which has been dipped into a jug of warm water. Comb through, from roots to points, taking care not to pull at the knots. Prepare the hair for pin-curling, by loosely forming waves. Take clean, neat sections, approximately 3 centimetres square. Pincurl, using flat barrelspring pincurls. Secure, using T pins.

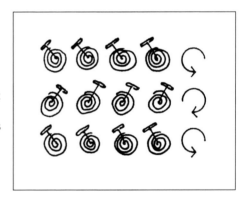

Flat/finger waving gives a long-lasting wave formation, shaped to the head

These waves are formed using the comb and the fingers. After each wave has been formed, it is held in position using fabric tape and postiche pins. Secure the wig onto a malleable block of the correct size, using postiche pins. Dampen the hair by shaking water from a comb which has been dipped into a jug of warm water. Comb through, from roots to points, taking care not to pull at the knots. Hold the comb with the three middle fingers on the top and the thumb and little finger underneath.

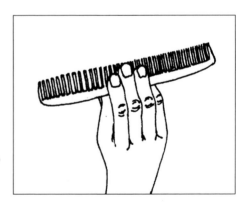

Form the first wave by creating a half circle. Place the first finger into the centre of the wave.
Place the comb beneath the finger at an angle.
Slide the comb across to form the crest.

Change the fingers over, so that the crest is held between the first and second fingers.

Form the next wave by combing the hair into the opposite direction and repeating the process in the opposite direction.

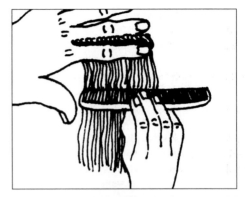

NB Every time the hair is combed through, the comb must be taken right to the points of the hair.

Secure each wave by placing tape over the centre and pinning with T pins.
In each case, the wig must be dried as before.

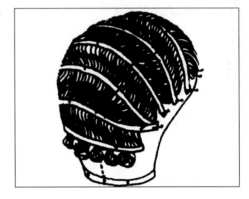

Dressing the waves
For the waves created using vertical rollers, the hair should be brushed to form the wave. Reverse pin-curls are brushed through, then combed into shape using the fingers and comb as one would for finger waving. Where a wig has been finger waved it only requires a light brushing.

Revision test
Without referring to the text or back to your notes, answer the following on a separate sheet.

1   Why is it necessary to set and dress hair?

2   Why is a workroom order form/record card used?

3   What type of hair spray must be used?

4   Why might a neutralising rinse be used?

5   When would you use tape in the setting of postiche?

6   List six precautions when setting and dressing postiche.

7   What specific precautions would you take when blow drying the hair?

8   Name the three different methods of putting a wave into the hair.

9   What is the main precaution when placing rollers into postiche?

10 How is the wig stored?

Lesson Twenty Five
Attaching postiche securely to the head
This section explains the different methods of attaching postiche. Each piece is fixed differently.

Equipment required (Items with codes are available at Banbury Postiche Ltd)

In addition to the cleansed and dressed postiche you will need one or more of the following:

Workroom order form
Combs (BD range)
Brushes (Denman range)
Grips (HS3000-12)
Pins (HS2000-2065)

Clips (PC2091)
Back mirror
Light hairspray
Toupee adhesive/tape or spirit gum (TA1050/TA1090)
Scalp cleanser/surgical spirit

The theory section should take at the most thirty minutes.
Follow this by completing the revision passage that follows, allowing fifteen minutes.

Attaching postiche
Each different type of postiche has its own method of application.

Have you ever worn a hairpiece?
Did you feel comfortable?

Have you ever been aware of a person wearing postiche?
If your answer was yes, then you were probably aware for one of two main reasons:

a   because you knew the wearer personally and so knew the length of the hair in its normal style

b   because the wearer was uncomfortable in the hairpiece.

The most important point which must be ensured is that the client feels comfortable in the postiche.
It should be part of him/herself. In fact, the client should not be able to feel that he/she
is wearing postiche.

The wig
After greeting the client and taking him/her to your work area, you must gown up to avoid any hairs or
spray etc falling onto the client's clothing. If the client has hair, then it should be brushed through, to
check the scalp for any cuts or abrasions and also to check that the hair and scalp are clean. It may be
necessary to shampoo and dry the hair before apply-ing the wig. If a client has long hair, then this must
be dressed up onto the crown of the head, using as few grips and pins as possible.

Attaching postiche to the head

The wig
As the wig is the piece of postiche that has the ability to completely transform a client's appearance, it
is often advisable to place the wig onto the head without the client being seated in front of a mirror.

The same rule would apply, even more so, if the wig were for a client under stress following an accident.
He or she can gain a terrific amount of confidence from seeing themself for the first time as they were.
Whereas if the client had watched the transformation then he/she would still see their head as it was
underneath – they are often unable to change the mental picture they have of themself.

Attaching

If the client has hair, for example if the wig is being used for a change for a party or the theatre, then the hair should be brushed through and taken away from the face.

Long hair should be taken up onto the crown – that is the reason for using caul/wig net – it stretches.

1 Remove the T pins and take the wig from the malleable block.

2 Hold at the centre front, using the finger and thumb.

3 Place this at the centre front of the head and hold firmly.

4 Gently ease the wig backwards, over the crown, towards the centre back, using the finger and thumb of the other hand.

5 Ease any hair which might be protruding, up under the wig using the tail of your comb.

6 Ensure that the fit is good. If you have altered the tension elastic it may require slight adjustment.

7 Check the workroom order form to ensure the style direction etc is correct.

8 Finally show the client the new 'look' from every angle.

If you have carried out all the requirements of the workroom order form, then the client will be satisfied.
If, for any reason the client is unhappy, then that must be rearranged at this point.
Before the client leaves the salon, explain the method for removing the wig and re-attaching it.
He/she will also need to be guided in the methods of storage and how to look after the wig.

NB Some clients like the wig to be gripped into position if they have existing hair. These grips are normally placed one on the crown and one either side, just in from the temple peak. The hair from the wig is then dressed over the top.

The toupee

Gown the client, to make sure that nothing can drip onto the clothing.
Prepare all the materials and equipment.

Method

1 Check the scalp for cuts and abrasions. If these are severe, there may be contra-indications.

2 Cleanse the scalp, using scalp cleanser or surgical spirit.
   This is to remove any grease or build-up of adhesive, therefore preventing discomfort.

3 Cut lengths of adhesive tape to the correct size for the adhesive patches and fix firmly to the adhesive patches on the toupee.

4 If using toupee adhesive or spirit gum, this is placed onto the adhesive patches.
   Great care must be taken not to overlap the designated area.

5 Beginning at the centre front and working across the crown to the furthermost point of the toupee, place onto the client's head.

6 Gentle but firm pressure must be used to ensure a good adhesion.

7 Dress the toupee in with the client's own hair.

8 Show the client the result from every angle, making sure he/she is satisfied.
   Make any changes necessary.

9   Explain the method of removal and re-application of the toupee.

10 Advise on the best methods of storage.

Wired weft (the diamond mesh)
This type of postiche is usually worn for adornment. Perhaps the client is going out to an evening event where dress is formal and she requires a more classical style.

Check the type of fastener and prepare your equipment accordingly.

Method

This piece of postiche may be attached before commencing the final dressing or inserted into the dressing as it takes shape on the client.
The postiche may be ready dressed or left to dress in with the style.

After gowning the client there are several ways of fixing the postiche.

1   If the postiche has a comb, then there are
    two main methods:

a   to make a large pincurl with lightly backcombed hair and
    slide the comb into this.

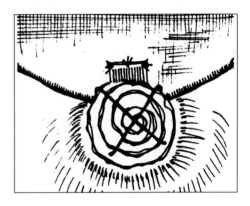

b   to backcomb the hair and slide the comb into the hair.
    Further grips and pins are positioned as necessary.

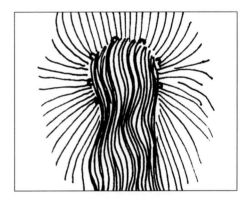

2   If the postiche has no comb, then it is attached
    directly to the hair.

a   Lightly backcomb the hair and make a large pincurl.
    Place grips around the perimeter to secure the postiche.

b   Metal roller pins can be used by inserting through the
    postiche. This is then twisted round and pushed forward,
    effectively tying a knot through the hair. The removal
    of the pin releases all the hair. Often only 4–6 pins
    are required.

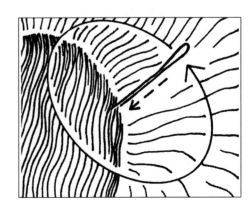

Finish the dressing on the client and show her the finished effect. Before she leaves the salon, explain the methods for removal and re-attaching in addition to the best method of storage.

Other types of postiche

The switch
This piece of postiche is finished with a loop.
A grip is pushed through the loop and into the client's hair before the style is dressed. It is sometimes preferable to use more than one grip.

The marteau
Two loops, one at each end, are used for attaching the marteau.
It is normally sufficient for one grip at each end.

Pincurls
These are attached by inserting a grip through the loop.

Torsades and double loop clusters
One loop is formed at either end of the postiche for attachment purposes.
A grip is inserted through each loop.

The main precautions to be remembered when fixing postiche are:

1   Do not use more pins, grips etc than are absolutely necessary.
    Although the postiche must be firm, using too many pins can make the result very heavy for the client.
2   Do not allow any pins etc to scratch the scalp.
3   Do not use toupee adhesive etc where there are cuts or abrasions.
4   Client comfort is important at all times.
5   The client must be advised as to the best methods of storage.

Revision test
Without referring back to your notes or to the text, supply the missing information in the following:

When attaching postiche, it is important to remember that -?- must be maintained throughout.

If the pins, grips etc are placed too firmly, then it may not only -?- the scalp, but could cause discomfort to the client.

A wig is placed onto the head beginning at the -?-.

Any stray pieces of hair are tucked in using your -?-.

-?- are used to attach a toupee.

These should not be used if -?-.

When attaching a wig to the head, some clients like extra security in the form of -?-.

These are placed -?-.
The name given to the areas of the toupee where the adhesive is placed is -?-.

Give five other types of postiche and the methods of attaching.
When attaching a wig following an accident, it is advisable to do this:
-?-

This is to avoid -?-

Lesson Twenty Six
Using boardwork for fun

In this section, I will show you how the art and craft of boardwork can be used to make fun pieces.

These can be sold at fetes and in some salons for extra income.

The theory part should take about 45 minutes to work through. The amount of time you spend on practical application depends upon the number and type of postiche you are making.

Boardwork purely for fun

How often have you been to a fete or a bazaar of some kind and hoped you could find some little item, completely out of the ordinary, as a small or extra present?

You have the knowledge now to make just such an item.
What sorts of items can be made for fun use?

Furry animals
Monsters!!!
Eyelashes
Hairy chests etc, etc

Furry animals

The limit of 'strange' animals that can be made depends on your imagination. Any shape or form can be fashioned.

Basic furry animals

1   Take some animal stuffing. This can be purchased from good dressmaking shops.

2   Place it inside an old piece of a pair of tights.

3   Mould it into the approximate shape of your finished animal.

4   You can stitch it into the shape if it helps.

5   Using a tape measure, make a pattern for the outer shape.
    Alternatively this pattern could be formed by lying cling film over and shaping to the 'animal'. Sello tape over the cling film carefully.

6   Gently remove from the shape. Cut, where necessary, to lie the pattern flat.

7   Place onto a base, preferably a rounded wooden shape (half circle).

8   Cover the pattern with net, allow it to extend 1cm all around the pattern, secure with block points.

9   Knot the area of the pattern.

10 Remove from the base.

11 Turn inside out and sew all the joins apart from one. Make sure it is large enough for the stuffing to be inserted.

12 Turn the foundation the right way round.

13 Insert the stuffing.

14 Sew the last join together using a lacing type stitch.

15 Gently brush the hair into the required direction.

16 Trim off where necessary.

17 Decorate with eyes etc as needed.

Suggested animals
Octopus, spider, bird, hedgehog, squirrel.
Although as I have already stated, the shapes possible are unlimited.

Eyelashes
If you go into one of the larger beauty salons or look on their price list, you will notice that the attaching of false eyelashes is mentioned.

The wearing of false eyelashes was very fashionable in the 1950's to 1960's.

False eyelashes can be purchased at chemists or department stores.

The cost depends upon the quality of the lashes.

Hand made human hair lashes are the most expensive.
For the experienced boardworker a pair of eyelashes is easy to make.

Benefits of hand made eyelashes

1	Lighter in weight	better for the tender skin around the eyes.
2	Size as needed	eg if only required at the outer edge of the lower lid.
3	Any colour	Hair can be bleached and tinted. Crazy colours for parties.
4	Length as required	Some clients ask for the lashes to be equal to their own. Others wish them to be extra long so that there is no doubting their falseness.

Method

1 Set up the weaving frame, using three lengths of silk thread.
2 Place the prepared hair, ie colour, into the drawing brushes.
3 Carry out a starting knot.
4 Weave the required amount in extremely fine thrice in weaving. This is normally 2.5cms to 3cms.
5 Finish with a finishing knot.
6 Cut down and tie a fine knot at each end. Alternatively, the ends can be fused together, using a tiny amount of beeswax.
7 Press with Marcel Irons to curl the lashes.

The lashes are attached to eyes using a special lash adhesive, available from chemists.

Hairy chests

These are shaped pieces of net which are knotted with short curly hair. The 'chests' are attached to the wearer by either a length of ribbon around the neck or by double-adhesive tape similar to toupee tape. It is preferable for this knotting to be double knotting on caul net.

Lesson Twenty Seven
Methods of advertising and techniques of selling

This section is designed to promote ideas for the selling of postiche.

It would be helpful for you to have a sketch pad and/or some tracing paper to hand.

Methods of advertising and techniques for selling

Let us first look at why it is necessary to advertise postiche.

Jot down any reasons you might think are relevant.

....

....

....

....

I do not know how many reasons you might have written, but if we look closely at them I am sure they will fall into two main categories.

Category one
To increase the turnover of the salon/wig boutique.

Category two
To increase the public's knowledge of products available.

Good advertising means more work for the wigmaker and the posticheur.
This means there is more income for the business.
The higher the income of the business the more the owner can promote the products of his/her business. The more promotion that a business has, the greater the awareness of the public to the services being offered.

If advertising is carried out tastefully then persons who had never thought of postiche begin to consider its possibilities.

It follows that if a business is advertised correctly, then it should give more work for the employees.

Most wigmakers are paid a basic salary plus commission. It is obvious, therefore, that the more work they have to do, the better their pay. Increased sales of wigs and hairpieces not only give work to the wigmaker, the posticheur will have more to do. Remember, each piece needs firstly to be measured and then after completion it requires to be cut and styled for the client.
Once clients have realised the value of postiche, they usually build up their wardrobe.

Where have you seen wigs/hairpieces advertised?

....

....

....

....

What are the best ways of advertising?
The best advertisement of all is word of mouth.
Unfortunately, though, unless the postiche is worn for adornment or
for fun, it is unlikely the client will advertise the fact that he/she is wearing postiche.

How can we overcome this?
If your staff wear wigs and let people know.
For example a member with long hair could wear a short wig.
When a comment is passed about having their hair cut, he/she would explain how they have the best of both worlds with wigs. Likewise a member with short hair could wear a long wig.

Styles changing from curly to straight and the other way around, also show how versatile postiche can be.

Most promotion takes the form of newspaper advertising or advertising in trade magazines. To get the most out of this form of advertising, enlist the services of a qualified designer. It is cost-effective to have all graphic material for a business in the same style and going to a professional is the only way to avoid drastic errors.

You would not expect a client for a wig to go to a dressmaker would you?

An interesting window display is another way of encouraging interest in your products. This should be changed frequently. There is nothing more off-putting than to see the same display from one year to the next.

Your posticheur should be employed to dress wigs out relative to the season, or to a recent happening in the news. Make your window interesting, so that members of the public notice you are there. That way they become interested in you and your products.

To visit local groups showing the versatility of postiche builds interest in postiche. Take a selection of postiche with you and hold a 'party' evening where prospective clients can try on postiche under the guidance of posticheurs. Offer a free styling with each purchase.

Promotional shows alongside either a hair salon or a fashion house give the public an insight into the products available and the services you can offer.

Promotion by video can reach a very wide audience. A good video can increase sales.

Techniques for selling
The staff involved in the selling of your products must be fully conversant with all the items on your stock list. This will make certain they can answer any questions that might arise and advise accordingly. Staff should be able to explain the differences between the types of postiche, the materials they are made from and the costs involved.

How to go about selling postiche

Be prepared to sit down with your clients and discuss their needs. The initial consultation will allow you to answer the main points for consideration. This area of your wig boutique/salon should be relaxed and informal. Most of all it should be comfortable so that a client relaxes.

Consider the reasons the client is thinking of postiche.
Why is it being bought? For fashion, for work, for fun or due to necessity?

If for fashion, then a sound knowledge of the current fashion trends is important.

It might be that a client requires a wig or hairpiece for work, as with models. This client needs advice on how to attach postiche, which will appear the more natural or outrageous as requested, in front of a camera.

110

Wigs are often purchased for fun.
Perhaps the client is going to a party or wishes to complete a fancy dress outfit.

If the postiche is being purchased out of necessity then much thought and discussion should go into the advice given.*

*When postiche is purchased following an accident or illness (where the treatment has caused loss of hair), it is extremely important to have private fitting rooms. Clients in this category are likely to be embarrassed at the situation in which they find themselves. A good posticheur is aware of the feelings of his/her client. Always use a sympathetic approach but do not be condescending in your attitude. Treat all clients with tact. Be discreet about their losses; they are confiding and therefore trusting you.

There are two main types of postiche: *human hair* and *synthetic fibre.*

Always present completed postiche in a dressed form. The wig/hairpiece looks nothing if it is pulled straight out of a box. The way an article is packaged/presented can make or break the sale.

Postiche made from human hair...
...hand made to the client's requirements so the cost is more than an off-the-shelf piece.

To offset the costs it is important to note the following:
Each piece is made to order so it fits comfortably.
The postiche is personally styled for the client.
Human hair lasts much longer than synthetic fibres.
Cutting and styling are more natural.

Human hair postiche must be cleansed and dressed professionally. These costs are to be considered.

Machine-made human hair postiche is available. This is mostly made in the Far East.
This type of postiche is superior to synthetic fibres but is not as natural as hand made postiche.

Postiche made from synthetic fibres...
...far cheaper than human hair postiche. It is available off-the-shelf, though it is not made for the individual. This type of postiche is made to be adjusted. Cleansing is carried out simply by washing it in a bowl of warm, soapy water. Most artificial fibres are antistatic. These are now available with a simulated cuticle to give a more natural feel to the hair. The postiche is made so that it can reflect light similar to the human hair. Most colours are available.

Problems
Will melt easily.
Can only be styled using steam.
Does not last as long as human hair postiche.
Sometimes has an artificial shine to the hair.
Synthetic fibres can increase the perspiration of the scalp.

Advertising and selling postiche
Without referring to the text or back to your notes, answer the following.

1   Give three reasons for advertising postiche.
2   List three main reasons for the purchase of postiche.
3   List four ways of promoting business.
4   Why is it necessary to advertise?
5   Why should staff know about all the products you are offering?
6   How would you go about advertising a new service offered by your boutique?

Lesson Twenty Eight
Health and safety

In this section I intend to concentrate on the safety aspects required when wigmaking.
We shall look at the reasons for the requirements and also the best methods of achieving them.
I would suggest that you take forty five to sixty minutes to work through the theory section.

Health and safety at work

Why are Health and Safety Acts of Parliament made?
The main reason is to ensure a safe environment for persons to work in.

What is meant by a safe environment?
A building or area which is as free from hazards as is possible.

What types of hazards could there be?
Health hazards, building hazards or equipment hazards.

What are health hazards?
Health hazards include anything that might cause illness to an employee.

Let us list the components of a safe working environment.

1   The facilities for washing one's hands etc when necessary.
2   Suitable toilet facilities. The law states the requirements, which relate to the number of employees
    and whether they are male or female.
3   Adequate first aid resources.
4   Correct lighting.
5   Good ventilation.
6   Control over the amount of fumes and dust that are allowed to permeate the atmosphere.
7   Regulated humidity.
8   Chemicals etc correctly stored.
9   Chemicals correctly identified.
10 Chemicals transported and positioned correctly.
11 Handling of solutions under supervision/appropriate conditions.
12 Disposal of chemicals under correct supervision.
13 An accident register for recording all accidents whether major or minor.
14 Equipment stored correctly.
15 Equipment maintained regularly.
16 Employee training under qualified tuition.
17 Qualified supervisors.
18 Easy access to information about the company.

Probably the most helpful part of any good working environment is to have a sound safety policy which
is reviewed regularly by members of the management and the employees.

Employers and employees each have their parts to play if safety is to be assured.

The employer is responsible for
the entrances and exits of the building;
the upkeep of the equipment;
the instigation of safe working methods;
the provision of protective clothing where necessary;
providing first aid facilities;
providing fire fighting equipment;
organising regular fire drills;
providing a healthy working environment.

What should an employee be prepared to undertake?

1   To take all reasonable care with their own health.
2   To consider their own safety and take the required safety precautions.
3   To know all the emergency procedures.
4   To have the safety of colleagues and clients uppermost in their minds.
5   To report all potential hazards
6   To remain alert and watchful at all times
7   Not to interfere with any equipment positioned f or health and safety
8   Not to tamper with the equipment positioned fro safety reasons
9   To keep their hygiene to a good standard

Good training means that staff:
can identify possible hazards
take appropriate action
will work safely;
will know the rules

What are the main causes of accidents?

Carelessness
This could be human carelessness
Lack of concentration
Not observing the rules
Fooling about

The wearing of the wrong clothing
Frills can be come caught
Overalls stop marks on clothing
Jewellery can cause accidents

Insufficient training
Attempting skilled work without the knowhow

Without enough experience
Can be dangerous

Lack of qualified supervision
Can lead to mistakes

Fatigue
Trying to work when overtired causes mistakes

Drunkenness
Working whilst influenced by drink is very dangerous particularly where machinery is concerned

Drugs
A person has no control over his or her actions whilst influenced by drugs

Surroundings
Untidy
Stops freedom of movement
Can trip persons up

Not cleaned correctly
Allows germs to breed
Unhealthy

Incorrect ventilation
Causes an unhealthy atmosphere
Can cause infection

Lighting
If the lighting is poor it can cause problems for staff,
eg headaches, eyesight

Space
Too many people in too small a space leads to an unhealthy atmosphere.
It also makes staff unhappy

Equipment
Stored incorrectly
Without guards
Near water if electrical

Badly maintained
Leads to faulty machinery
Can cause accidents

It is extremely important that all such accidents be avoided

Therefore what measures should be taken to prevent accidents?

1 Always replace guards on machinery and tools.
2 Check electrical plugs and leads before each use.
3 Check all equipment is earthed correctly.
4 Use portable equipment correctly.
5 Remove any items which may cause accidents.
6 Change to safer methods.
7 Work sensibly.
8 Wear the correct clothing.
9 Follow the company rules and regulation at all times.
10 Report potential hazards.
11 Don't drink alcohol whilst operating machinery.
12 Do not take drugs.

Working with the chemicals that we d, all staff should be made aware of the correct methods of...

Fighting fires
Most fire stations have officers trained to inform the general public what to do in the event of a fire.
It is always beneficial to request the services of an expert

They will explain how fires can start.
Cigarette ends left burning near rubbish, etc.
Chemicals incorrectly stored or used.
Faulty electrical equipment.

There are many, many more reasons why fires start.

Fire spreads rapidly, always working upwards.
Fire needs something on which to feed, eg rubbish and oxygen.
Starve it of these and you will put out the fire.
This must be carried out correctly.
If you use the wrong extinguisher you can compound the problem.

General rules

Water or foam extinguishers
Do not use on electrical fires

Carbon dioxide gas extinguishers
Can be used on electrical fires

Carbon dioxide foam
Do not use on electrical fires.

Dry powder extinguishers
Can be used on electrical fire

Fir blankets
Thrown over a fire will smother it

Sand buckets
Can be used on electrical fires if electricity has been turned off

Of course, all necessary precautions should be taken to prevent fires.

Do not smoke near chemicals or in an inappropriate place.
Replace any frayed electrical wires
Use the correct fuse size
Maintain all electrical equipment regularly.
Do not allow rubbish to accumulate incorrectly
Store chemical wisely

The Fire Precautions Act (1971) is the act of Parliament relevant to this area of safety.
It is normally the job of the local fire brigade to see that this is obeyed.

Amongst other items, the act covers
the provision of clear and unlocked exits in case of fire;
the suitability of extinguishers and that they are maintained;
the fire certificate which must be obtained where either more than ten persons work on one floor or where more than twenty people work.

General rules for a safe and hygienic working environment

Keep all surfaces clean and free from germs.
Sweep up all hair fro m the floor as each job is completed.
Store this hair in a covered container.
Maintain your own personal hygiene.
Ensure good ventilation
Use sterilisation cabinets
Wash hands before and after attending to a client, even if only measuring
Use clean towels and gowns
Cover all cuts.
Store equipment correctly
Keep all hair to be used in boardwork, in mothproof container.
Store chemicals correctly
Mix chemicals correctly
Take all necessary precautions.
Tale all necessary tests to establish if the client is allergic to such things as spirit gum or the synthetics fibres sometimes used.
Treat all equipment with care, thus avoiding accidents.
Ensure that the first aid box is kept well stocked.

In this industry, electrical equipment is used frequently. It is important for staff to know that the human body can form part of an electrical circuit if safety precautions are not adhered to.

The main precautions are
to use dry hands
to work where there are no pipes or water;
to handle correctly.

Where an accident happens, causing an electrical shock, there are several procedures to be taken

1 Switch off the power immediately.

2 Move the patient away from the electricity.
   If you have not been able to stop the electricity, then use a wooden handle
   or a pair of rubber gloves

3 Summon professional help.

4 If the heart has stopped it will necessary to carry out artificial respiration
   Mouth to mouth is the most usual method used.
   Another way to attempt to make the heart beat again by pressing down on the sternum(breastbone)
   with one hand on top of the other. This should only be carried out after professional tuition.

5 Treat for burns if necessary.
   Cover with a sterile dressing.
   If the burns are severe they should be treated professional.

6 Electrical shocks can trigger off an epileptic fit.
   Treatments vary.
   All state to remove furniture from around the patient.
   Some say to place a pencil between the teeth whilst others say not to.
   The patient will come out of the fit most likely requiring a rest.
   Before treating any accident victims, be sure you know what you are doing.
   In larger organisations it is advisable to have a trained member of staff

Lesson Twenty Nine
Legal Requirements

In this section, I will endeavour to outline, briefly, areas of the law, which relate to the working environments in which you may find yourself.

Spend about forty-five minutes on this section.

Legal Requirements
Law is a specialist profession. I intend to indicate the contents of the acts. If you should decide to open a business you should consult the experts for help.

Offices, Shops and Railway Premises Act (1963)
You will normally find a shortened version of this act displayed in larger companies. You will, in most cases, be able to see a copy if you wish. Basic health and safety regulations are specified in the act.

For example, it
states the number of toilets
explains the washing facilities required;
states the need for a suitable area for eating;
says that the lighting must be adequate;
gives the regulations regarding floor space;
gives requirements for working temperatures;
states that the space must be allowed for hanging up wet clothing;
explains the space which must be allowed per person.

Factories Act 1961
The Factories Act covers more than just factories.
It includes warehouse, dockyards, papermaking and printing firms, laundries, garages,
works and many more.

Details of the requirements of this act can obtained from the Health and Safety Inspector. The Factories Act requires;
floors, passageways and stairs must not be obstructed;
floors etc must not be slippery;
equipment like ropes and lifts must be correctly maintained;
all fences to be properly looked after;
that enough toilet and washing facilities must be provided;
good ventilation;
correct lighting;
plus many other rules which make a safer working environment.

The Health and Safety Act 1974
This was designed to update the Offices, Shops and Railway Premises Act of 1963. It does not completely replace it though.
This act identifies the general health and safety responsibilities of the employer and the employee. It refers to first aid requirements.

How the Act is enforced
Health and Safety
Employers responsible for;
storing materials correctly;
ensuring the work place is safe;
safety instruction for staff;
correct care and maintenance of equipment;
producing a health and safety policy for the workforce where there are more than five employees.

117

The employee is responsible for following the guidelines of the employer's health and safety policy, for example
clothes worn;
method of work;
places to eat or smoke;
reporting of hazards etc;
taking reasonable care of his/her own health and safety;
taking care that his/her actions do not injure others.

The provision of a first aid kit is a necessity of the Act.
It gives guidelines as to what should be included in the kit.

Regulations relating to the reporting of accidents are also included in this act. All incidents and the resulting injuries must be written down.

The law is enforced by Health and Safety Inspectors.
They can order improvements to the workplace.
They can stop the use of equipment they consider dangerous.
They can stop premises being used if they are unsuitable

Safety at work is also included in other documents such as
Safety representatives and Safety Committees 1977;
Notification of Accidents and General Occurrences Regulation 1980;
The Fire precautions Act of 1971 was mentioned in the preceding section of Health and Safety.

Employers Liability (Compulsory Insurance) Act 1969
This covers the requirement of the employer to take out correct insurance.
The insurance should cover the accidents to themselves, their staff and their clients.

I have only touched the surface of the legal requirements.
Remember that if you decide to open a business you should consult the expert.

Lesson Thirty
The History

In this section, I hope to explain briefly the way postiche has developed throughout the years. We shall look at who wore postiche, why they wore it and what it was like.

This section is intended only as an insight into the history.

For deeper knowledge, visit your library.
Amongst the many books which give such information are:
The Strange Story of False Hair, John Woodforde
A History of Women's Hairstyles 1500-1965, Jean Keyes
Hairstyles and Headdresses, Renee Huggett

Many encyclopedias and other books on hairstyles and fashion mention pastiche as it relates to the topic of the book.

Everytime we go to a museum, investigate old buildings like the pyramids we see evidence of wigs being used in history. When watching historic films or television, whether they are factual or fictional, there is evidence that the historians have proof of artificial coverings for the head being worn for a long while. Amongst the ancient cultures who were known to wear wigs were the Assyrians, Egyptians, Greeks, Persians and Romans.

In the early Egyptian times, heads were mostly shaved.
This was either for religious reasons or for hygienic purposes.
As the climate was very hot, it was considered more healthy to allow the scalp more freedom.

So, why did they wear wigs?
1   To show their position in society
    The higher up they progressed, the bigger the wig.
2   Headdresses were worn by persons in the religious orders
    Different headdresses denoted different positions
3   Wigs were worn to protect the scalp from the heat of the sun
4   The Egyptians also wore wigs because they believed that it would placate the Gods.

What were wigs made from ?
Animal Wool
Animal Hair
Leaves – for example, palm leaves which were split into their fibres before being made into headdresses.
Materials like gold and silver were included in the headgear of the pharaohs.
Skins like leather.
Hair was used but only in the later stages.
In fact there was very little attempt to imitate hair for a long while.

What were the wigs like?
Rulers had wigs which were very expensive and ornate.
The usual design had a theme based on one of their gods
Gold and Silver were often included in these wigs.
The more expensive, the more the ruler liked it.

High officials wore large wigs.
These would be braided or have spiral curls.
Materials used would be according to their position.

As you worked down the ladder, the wigs became smaller.
The ordinary man would wear a skull cap made of leather or felt.
Sometimes a man would go about with no covering on his head, risking the heat of the sun on his scalp.

Young boys would shave their heads.
Locks of hair would then be fixed to the sides of their heads. These were called 'locks of youth'.

Female wigs
These tended to be flat at the top, with braids hanging down to below the shoulders.

Again, the more important a female, the more expensive and ornate the wig.

Points relating to the wigs themselves
They had mesh-type base to allow the air to circulate.
The style formed by the hair of fibres was held in position using beeswax.
When we see pictures portraying Egyptian wigs they always look very shiny. To gain this effect a pomade of perfumed fat was place on the top of the wig.
As the wearer went about daily business, the heat of the sun caused the wax to melt and coat the wig.
The wig would then keep its shape, look shiny and smell nice.

What colours were used?
Mostly the colour was black, the fibres being dyed by natural plant extracts. There are records, though, that some people wore vivid greens, blues and reds. Even the occasional blonde.

Styles
These did not change much. Pictures which we see show all the head dresses and styles for wigs, similar over a period extending from 3000BC t0 1805BC.
Fringes did appear around 1500BC but only attached to a few wigs.

What other types of postiche were worn?
Facial pastiche was widely worn by males. Again, this was not made solely of hair. Precious metals were also used. The beard could be attached to the wig, making the shape similar to a balaclava.

Mesopotamian civilization
These wore very elaborate dressings. They were mostly spiral curls or long wavy styles.

Sometimes very tight ringlets were included.
When we talk about 'frizzing' hair we are using a word derived from a word used by persons from Phrygia in Asia Minor – Phrygianize – meaning to frizzle or curl up.

Due to their love of ornate things they would powder their wigs with gold dust or scented dust for special occasions.

Their queens are depicted wearing very tall, crown-like headdresses.

Sovereigns also wore false beards made of metal.
Gold was the metal used most often for these pieces.
These beards were worn by queens as well as kings.
Later as they wore their own beards, plaited, they would treat them with gold dust and
wear a gold chin strap.

The Babylonian soldiers stated as being the first to wear helmets.
These were worn over the top of their wigs.

Beards were very important to the Babylonian people.
They were square in formation.
Very exquisitely designed.
Rows of spiral curl going in different directions.

Greek cultures wore their heads adorned with wreaths of flowers. As before if they were high in society or a ruler then precious jewels or gold and silver metals were mingled into the wreath.
The Greeks wore wigs for adornment.
They also wore wigs to disguise themselves in battle.

What were their wigs like?
They were designed to frame the face, enhancing the features.

Lots of single curls, sometimes spirally formed, were fixed to a wire base.
The curls were positioned to frame the face.

Laurel leaves were used to make crowns.
They were used to crown visitors.
Later they were used to crown people who had gained academic honours.

Feminine wigs and hairpieces.
These tended to combine different disciplines. Waves and spiral curls were combined. The back of the head shaped to stand out from the head. Ornamentation like flowers or ribbons formed an integral part of these wigs. The wire frames sometimes just fitted from ear to ear across the front hairline.

Colours used
Greek women usually had natural blonde hair. They often dyed their own hair. Favourite colour was red. (It is written that Athenian women dyed their hair blue then dusted it with gold or silver.) Greek people used wigs extensively in the theatre. Greek theatre was almost totally male dominated, so wigs were worn to indicate a change of sex.

The Romans thought that the baldness was some kind of deformity. So the men who were unfortunate enough to lose their hair would have a wig made. These were made from hair stuck to the scalp.

The Roman man was not too keen on the femininity of the Greek wigs. They tended towards more basic styles. They did not wear a parting. It was customary for the to be dressed from central point on the crown. It was then allowed to fall loosely towards the hairline.

It is reported that some bald men did not wear wigs but painted their scalps instead. The Roman man who worked outside would wear a skull cap of animal skin.

The Roman women, on the other hand, loved ornate wigs. They had slaves just to attend to their coiffure. These wigs frequently had a centre parting. The hair was dresses in tight crimp like forms. It was then tied back on the crown or the nape. Jewellery, ribbons, flowers etc finished off the style. Their choice of colour was usually red or brown. They loved the golden and flaxen blondes. This had to be chosen with great care as yellow hair was linked with women of ill repute.

As we go through history, we can see how the ideas of the rulers and the church determined the wearing of false hair or not. One report states that in the first century AD it was believed that no blessing given by a priest which involved the laying on of hands, would pass through the wig to the wearer.

In the second century AD wearing of anything 'false' was frowned upon. You did not know where the hair had come from! That person could have been a sinner! One archbishop of an English cathedral is said to have allowed no-one with long hair, real or false in his cathedral. This was because long hair was linked with sin at this time.

During the centuries that followed, the fashion for wearing wigs was dictated strongly by the church and royalty. It fluctuated greatly. The sixteenth century had styles for women where their hair was dressed over pads to build it up high.

Their obsession with large collars determined that the hair was dresses up away from the face. Wire frames were fixed to the head to give various shapes and a more rigid base for the hair to be dressed.

Frequently we see pictures showing that pearls and other jewels were used to adhorn these dressings.

Some women, who found the length of time require by a hairdresser tedious, would have wigs made to save them bother.

There are reports that Queen Elizabeth I has as many as eighty wigs. Her favourite colours were red and yellow (saffron). As a mark of respect for the Queen, women wear their wigs dyed red.

History shows that at this time a piece of postiche which covered the whole head was called a periwig.

Smaller pieces of pastiche like ringlets were also called wigs.

In the seventeenth century, men wore very full, long wigs. They were waved and curled to fall loosely on the shoulders from central parting. Powder, not wax was used.

Men wore far more 'glamorous' wigs than the women. (In fact women are recorded a swearing only part wigs. The full wig which was worn was the riding wig.)

Hats, decked with feathers, complemented the hairdressing.

Types of wigs
The full-bottomed wig was the favourite of men in high office.
The travelling wig, an adapted full-bottomed wig, was tied back into a queue (hair braided at the back.)

Tradesmen wore a bobbed wig which was shorter than the full-bottomed wig.

Professional men, doctors and barristers, wore wigs to denote their importance.

The campaign wig was dresses into two curls which hung either down the back or over the shoulder of travellers and soldiers. There was a short bob wig of curls which was also worn by soldiers and travelling men

Another piece worn during the first half of this century was the lovelock. This was a long curl which hung down the left side of the face. Of course, we hear of Cromwell's roundheads. For about ten years their hair was styled short with a fringe.

After this, the coiffures reverted back to their original elegance.
Women wore a longer curl than the lovelock; it was termed the heart breaker. The lock hung down as far as the neck. The styles were sometimes given lift and shape by being laid over a wire frame. Several heart breakers would be attached to the perimeter of a style.

The latter part of the century saw wigs as a symbol of wealth and authority. The bigger the wig, the more important the person.

At the end of the seventeenth century, wigs were so big and bulky that hats could not have been worn. The colours used were normally just black and brown, to imitate hair such as possible.

The beginning of the eighteenth century saw women wearing very simple styles.
Men wore the full-bottomed wig for the first twenty years.
After that, it was only the elderly and professional men who used wigs.

Types of wigs
The tye or tie-wig where the hair was drawn back and tied with a black silk ribbon was worn by young men.

The bag wig was first worn by soldiers.
The hair was enclosed in a black taffeta bag at the nape.
This material was gummed to make it stiff.

A string threaded through the top of the bag allowed it to be drawn together. The tie was decorated with a bow or rosette. Later this wig was worn by many men. Around 1740 the bags became larger, they protected the coat from the powder and grease used on the wigs.

The pigtail wig was worn by soldiers and sailors.
It had one or two tight braids, bound spirally with black ribbon.

The paint brush was like a pigtail.
The difference was that these pigtails, queues or whips were not always made of hair. Leather or chamois had a tuft of hair stuck on the bottom.
They required polishing at the same time as their boots were done.

The Ramillies wig.
The tail of this wig had black ribbon tied at the top and bottom. The braid could be looped under and fastened with a ribbon.

The short, bushy bob wig was worn by the clergy.

The Cadogan wig (sometimes called the club wig).
The style was to loop the hair up the fasten it with string or black solitaire. Occasionally, it was held in place by a small comb.
Ladies would enclose the hair in a silk net.

The Adonis wig.
Very fashionable.
Made of pure white hair.

The brown wig.
Not particularly like. The brown powder dusted over used to cover the clothing as well.

The macaroni wig.
More of a headdress. It was stuffed with horse hair and wool.
The hair was dressed into a very large knot of hair at the back.

Cork wigs.
Fitted closely to the scalp, which was why they were termed cork. They did not contain any cork. They were very neat wigs.

The bob wig.
Several different lengths were made. Probably the most popular shot wigs without queues. The cauliflower bob was worn by doctors and clergymen. The long bob covered the whole of the nape. The short bob stopped just before the nape.

The physical or lion wig.
The hair was drawn back to the crown. The hair was then fluffed out and then moulded to the nape.

The scratch wig.
Was worn by farmers. Quite a small and disorganised wig. It did not cover the whole of the head. It was made so that the wearer could scratch his head underneath.

The clipped wig worn by servants.
One of the simplest of the wigs. Some farmers wore clipped wigs

The Brutus wig.
This wig was brown and always untidy.

Women in the eighteenth century had some very extravagant wigs. They were higher than before. They were more padded than before.

The wigs had long curls placed horizontally at the sides and back.
Ornaments were added. The wigs grew higher and lower at the same time.

Themes were used;
Animals like lions, tigers, bears etc.
Birds like the peacock, swan, Friesland hen.
Ostrich feathers decorated the wigs.
Garden scenes. One even had a working waterfall.
Real flowers were used.
Models of ships etc.
Any item to celebrate.
Fruit gardens.

Wig dressings were sometimes most absurd.

Towards the end of the eighteenth century a sense of normality returned to wigs. One of the last recorded wigs of this period was a bandeau with curls attached to it.

The nineteenth century brought transformation.

Shorter hair was worn.
If the hair remained long it was tied back in a chignon.
False hair was mixed in with a person's own hair.
The styles were quite angular. Some very unusual angles were used.
They contained curls and ringlets. Some decoration was used often in the form of pearls or beads.
Ribbons have also been used. Young girls would look like gifts. Bundles of curls would be tied up in bows and allowed to hang over the face.

Occasionally, the styles were dressed high to imitate previous styles. Styles developed a simplicity. They were flat on the crown area. Plaits of hair were wound round at the back. This chignon has been around in various form ever since.

In the nineteenth century, men wore wigs for baldness rather than for adornment.

Of course wigs were worn by both sexes in the theatre.

The method of making added hair had developed considerably. A fine lace or net base was used. Hair was knotted onto the base, therefore postiche was more natural looking. Human hair was the most popular material used for postiche.

During the twentieth century, wigs and added hair experienced some popularity.

Between the two wars, women would wear hats which had hair fixed at the nape. This was to cover up their own shingled hair.

After the second war, this developed into the use of small curls.
These could be single curls used for added interest or cluster of curls clipped into position on the head to make the hair appear long and tied up.

Synthetic hair was introduced into wig making.

Although this was not always as natural looking as real hair, it did bring down the price considerably.

Wigs became available on the National Health. Recognition that physical and mental traumas could result in hair loss.

Wigs were now made in various ways:

Hand knotted onto a net base.
Hand wefted then stitched onto a net base
Machine made – less natural looking that the other two but far cheaper.

Fun wigs were worn. This is where nylon is coloured vividly. Used for startling effect.

In the middle of the twentieth century, the wearing of wigs was the height of fashion. A variety of wigs and hairpieces was an important part of a women's wardrobe.

She would have wigs to match her outfits – even wigs for different moods.

There were wigs made to match the popular car colours.

Wigs were sold in the mid sixties as unisex wigs. Male and female styles were so alike at that time.

In more recent times, the postiche that is made is so natural that it is extremely hair to detect. Therefore the practice of wearing added hair is much wider than is commonly thought. Hairstylists are becoming more and more efficient at disguising the added hair within the wearer's own hair.

The wearing of added hair has been around for a long, long time. It has been influenced by changes in fashion, religious orders, the fads of kings and queens and social pressures.

I have every confidence that it will not go away. Added hair will always be required in one form or another.

Fashionable post-Restoration wig.

Ramillies wig, 18th centrury.

Powdered bag wig with pigeons' wings, 1728.

Ancient Egyptian king.

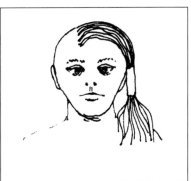
Ancient Egyptianboy with shaven head.

Ancient Egyptian high official.

Full-bottomed black wig,
English, c1670.

English, late 16th century.

Wig for professional men,
English, 1790.

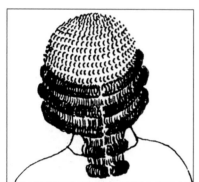

French wig 1761.

Bishop Thomas.

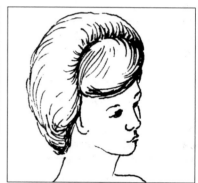

Half wig, 1959.

Banbury Postiche Ltd
Little Bourton House
Southam Road
Banbury
OX16 1SR

Tel: 01295 757 406
Fax: 01295 757 401

For supplies
www.banburypostiche.co.uk

For wigs
www.purelywigs.co.uk

For extensions
www.rapture-professional.co.uk